D1012359

CRYSTALS

A
CONSCIOUS
GUIDE

KATIE-JANE WRIGHT

CRYSTALS

How to tap into your infinite
potential through the healing
power of crystals

aster

I dedicate this book to my son – Arlo may you always "feel" the magic within you. And to my grandmother Catherine for supporting me down this path and passing on your healing hands to me.

An Hachette UK Company
www.hachette.co.uk

First published in Great Britain in 2018 by Aster, an imprint of
Octopus Publishing Group Ltd
Carmelite House
50 Victoria Embankment
London EC4Y 0DZ
www.octopusbooks.co.uk

Layout and Design Copyright © Octopus Publishing Limited 2018
Copyright © Katie-Jane Wright 2018

Distributed in the US by
Hachette Book Group
1290 Avenue of the Americas
4th and 5th Floors
New York, NY 10104

Distributed in Canada by
Canadian Manda Group
664 Annette St.
Toronto, Ontario, Canada M6S 2C8

All rights reserved. No part of this work may be reproduced or utilized in any form or by any means, electronic or mechanical, including photocopying, recording or by any information storage and retrieval system, without the prior written permission of the publisher.

Katie-Jane Wright asserts the moral right to be identified as the author of this work.

ISBN 978-1-9120-2394-3

A CIP catalogue record for this book is available from the British Library.

Printed and bound in China

10 9 8 7 6 5 4 3 2 1

Consultant Publisher: Kate Adams
Junior Editor: Sarah Vaughan
Copy Editor: Marion Paull
Art Director: Juliette Norsworthy
Illustration: Ella McLean
Design: Rosamund Saunders
Production Manager: Lisa Pinnell

No medical claims are made for the crystals in this book and the information given is not intended to act as a substitute for medical treatment.

The healing properties are given for guidance only and are, for the most part, based on anecdotal evidence and/or traditional therapeutic use. If in any doubt, a crystal healing practitioner should be consulted. In the context of this book, illness is a disease, the final manifestation of spiritual, environmental, psychological, karmic, emotional or mental imbalance or distress. Healing means bringing mind, body and spirit back into balance and facilitating evolution for the soul; it does not imply a cure. In accordance with crystal healing consensus, all crystals are referred to as crystals regardless of whether or not they have a crystalline structure.

Contents

Introduction

Crystalline awakening

What moves you? What makes your heart quicken, skip a beat?
Mine is connection and love, pure love aligning with my purpose.
I have such a passion, a gentle fire within to make a change to
someone, to guide people toward their truth with these
sensitive crystalline teachers, to feel the confidence to speak
from their heart and honour their soul.

This is not just me. I am more than this.

I am a thousand sparkling fireflies flying on a dark night,

I am the sky, the moon, the sun and all the stars.

I am made of the earth and my roots spread up and out
to the universe.

I am made of energy, subtle vibrations, every cell, every
part of my being vibrating, in constant flow.

Hundreds of golden cords reaching out and connecting
to everything that is and everything that ever was.

I am everything and everything is me,

And, my dear friend, so are you.

You are capable of everything and anything because you
have that same universe inside of you.

Katie-Jane

My journey with crystals so far

I have felt different all of my life. As I grew up I put a bubble around myself to protect my heart, after experiencing personal trauma and loss. When I was a child I saw and sensed spirits, or energy as I like to call it. I saw spirits with my third eye as if they were in front of me as clear as day. I saw and worked with energy orbs and when I focused my intention on one, I saw the air around me vibrate as if I saw every particle shaking. I could touch objects and see their past, and even meet spirits through them. Later I learned this is called psychometry.

My grandmother and our ancestry have deeply impacted my path, for it was through her that I received my healing hands. She was the one person who encouraged me down this path, asking me what I saw, never doubting what I said. She comes from a Khasie hill tribe in Northern India, a matriarchal culture where the women were strong, powerful earth mothers, in charge. They knew who they were.

But then, in my 20s, I shut out my psychic senses, along with a lot of other things, through not feeling worthy. This period in my life was spent comfortably numb; looking back, I was really lost. I had blinkers on and I thought life was so much easier if I just drifted through. I was not loving in the ways I should have been, and not accepting of the right love because I didn't think I deserved it.

A glimmer of light appeared when I reached my late 20s – my gifts just could not be suppressed any longer. Some things, we have to accept, are bigger than we are. When I tuned in to people, I started to see past lives through far vision. I saw the important moments of that life, karmic debt, patterns emerging and I just knew how to help them. I saw their blockages as knives, ropes and bullets in their aura and I learned intuitively how to take them out and work on the emotional body to support the healing process. I started to channel people's spirit guides through automatic writing and trance mediumship.

This happened very suddenly and was a scary thing at first. I had to learn how to let go of doubts or fears and let it be. I believe surrender and release are things we all have to work on. It turns out that this is what I can do to help people. I am an activator, an open channel closely linked to cosmic consciousness and awakening people to higher frequencies.

Now, I do not want to overwhelm and you may be new to crystals, but I am aware of a new crystal awakening and a thirst to learn, which leads me to the present day and this moment in which you have chosen to open yourselves up to the possibility that crystals can work for you. It might have been a conscious or unconscious decision, or it could have been unfolding for you just as it should and I have come to you to activate a new way of listening to your heart. Whichever it is, I am honoured you chose me and this book to support you. It is all I want, to use all the experience I have gathered with crystals and my energy work over the past few years to share with and empower you. I am just a coach, here to hold your hand. You are the real healer.

My spiritual path has been slowly unfolding over the past four years and these beautiful crystals have supported me, strengthened my intuition and brought a beautiful connection to my soul, and a deep peace that I could not have imagined was possible. I choose to help people with their awakening, building their intuition using crystals, because if I can build this connection without any formal qualifications, so can you. If you trust me to support you and assist you on this journey, my heart is here for you.

This book is a guide, it's my story, and it is a tool with which you might explore and deepen your own connection. Take the meditations and exercises that resonate with you to help you find awareness. Not all exercises work for everyone and it's important to know that we all have our unique ways of working with crystals. I want to help you discover your own. So please, add to my meditations and prompts, build on them, turn them into something that works for you and share them. Please share them.

A new age of crystal healing

It seems to me that a new age of crystal healing and crystal consciousness is dawning as more people are becoming aware of crystalline energy. You can hardly flick through a magazine without noticing crystals being mentioned in the lifestyle and beauty sections, used in interior shots, infused in facial oils and tonics, and used in massages and treatments.

You may have found yourself drawn to crystals for a number of reasons. Perhaps you were given a piece of jewellery made with your birthstone, you found yourself at a crystal healing workshop or you simply felt intrigued by the idea that crystals can work with our own energy in some way.

This new wave involves a much more intuitive way of working with crystals, channelled from spirit and remembered from our ancestors' time. Much ancient wisdom and knowledge of the mineral kingdom are coming back into the world. At the same time there is a strong rise in the use of plant medicine, which goes hand in hand with crystal healing.

Why do we need crystals?

Crystals amplify and raise energy vibrations, whether it's for you, your space, the land, even your pets. They can help us experience a greater awareness of our own energy. They offer a helping hand to keep us present and in the moment, which, let's face it, is much needed. They transmute energy and send ripples of good vibrations out into the space outside of you and within you. They help you to make change in your life.

Crystals help to balance our own energy system, and we will explore crystals and the chakras in a later chapter (Time to Tune In, page 52). They can generate just the right amount of universal life energy to support us when we are blocked, feel slowed down or in need of calming.

Do crystals *really* heal?

This is a question I am often asked. I cannot offer scientific proof as I am an intuitive healer and lead with my heart, which is how I choose to teach. On matters such as this I "feel", I do not think. I ask this question in return: "Do *you* feel they heal?" If you trust and are open, then yes, I know that crystals can be a magnificent tool to help you. Just keeping a piece of clear quartz in your pocket can expand your aura and raise your vibrations – in essence, make you feel GOOD!

I say "tool" because you already have everything you need inside of you. Crystals can help you to meet the clarity, connection, love, hope, peace and understanding that already exists within you. They can support your rituals, cleanse spaces and your energy systems. They can work as gently as they need to, to help you release what you need to release, and at the right time. And they can do all of this just by being in the same room with you once you have connected with them and asked them to work with you.

Crystal wisdom

There are two types of beautiful souls. The ones that are analytical like to know everything before they see or try it; they tend to do a lot of research. The others, those who just feel, do not need to know the why – they experience and see what they find. I would like to address both, but I really want you to use your intuition, the soft, gentle voice that comes from your heart. I would love you to start to dissent from the voice that comes from your head, your inner critic, the sceptic, the one that questions and always second guesses. If you sit quietly to become aware of your thoughts and feeling as often as you can, you will hear and feel the difference.

Working with crystals is about using your heart and not your mind. It is a very individual thing. Some people love to surround themselves with many crystals, enjoying all of the crystalline energy around them, while others need just one or two. Your preference can change during different cycles of your life. One of my favourite things to do is to keep a small bowl of tumble stones (small and polished rocks or minerals) in my hallway and reach for one before I leave the house. I see which jumps into my hand or calls to me.

During your lifetime, many different crystals will come to you at various times for different reasons and purposes. For years I was never drawn to rose quartz, and I didn't understand why. It's beautiful and gentle and almost everyone I knew had a piece. And then it called to me. I saw it in a dream and understood that until then I hadn't been ready to explore giving myself the kind of love I needed, a nurturing kind of love, very motherly, just like the crystal. Have a look at the crystals you have around you or what you feel drawn to. What do they say about you and what you need right now?

Crystals are tools to aid in our healing on a spiritual, emotional or physical level. They sometimes come to us via mysterious ways and leave just as fast. A lot of the time I know when a crystal has done its job with me and I pass it on to someone else who needs it. We are just guardians of these stones.

CRYSTAL MATES

Certain crystals that come to us totally match and resonate with our energy as if we were that crystal. I have matched a few people to their crystal mates and it's a lovely magical connection, which lights up both the new owner and the crystal. These crystals have much personal significance and are capable of helping that person for life, a tool for self-growth and self-healing. I connected a lady to a beautiful piece of lemon quartz, and I could see and feel the same aura around her and the crystal. Their energy was just a perfect match – bright yellow, full of sunshine and so uplifting. I really felt the sacredness of that connection. You will feel a similar strong magnetic connection to a crystal that is your crystal mate.

PART 1

Getting Started

What to consider when buying a crystal

Everyone who touches, holds or is around a crystal imprints energy onto it, whether positive or negative. Imagine how long that chain of people is before the crystal even reaches your hands. From the person who took it from the ground to those who received it, bought and sold it, packaged it – the list goes on. This is why it is always good to get into the habit of cleansing your crystals as soon as you get them home (page 32).

Even the land and the way the crystals are taken from it can affect their energy. A crystal mined from a war-torn area will retain the trauma of that environment and an imprint of the energy from the land. So it is important to know where your crystals come from, and if they were mined ethically. You can ask whoever you are buying from this question, but you will get to a point where that is not necessary – you will just feel it in the crystals, see it in their auras. You will know how healthy and happy they are from looking at them. A healthy, happy crystal shines compared with a sad, mistreated one.

Once mined, the cleaning processes crystals go through are many and varied. For example, some big pieces of Brazilian quartz are bathed in acid to remove the dirt and dust. You can imagine my horror when I learned that. I have seen people dye their crystals, amethyst in particular to make it more purple. The telltale is when the dye rubs off on your hands. I have also come across sellers who oil their crystals to make them shiny.

I held a crystal recently from a mine in Madagascar. It was sad and traumatized and showed me the way it had been pulled out of the earth, so roughly that a lot of its points had been splintered off. I felt its pain and shock and just had to save it. It shows you that crystals can hold on to traumatic memories and need TLC, just like us. They are sensitive beings. Sadly, for a lot of dealers the buying and selling of crystals is just business, but for us more used to the energetic side of things, it's different.

Who should you buy from?

Crystals are widely available – you can find them not just in specialist and metaphysical shops but also in interior and lifestyle stores and fashion boutiques – and with so much choice it's important to find a seller with whose energy you connect. If you can, buy from someone who resonates with some part of you; someone who seems to know what he or she is talking about, who speaks with passion and interest; someone who displays the crystals with care. Then you will know that the seller has been looking after the crystals in the right way.

Sometimes, though, a crystal will just call to you and you will have a deep need to buy it, regardless of the seller. This crystal is meant to be with you, so just go with it.

QUESTIONS TO ASK A SELLER

✴ **WHERE IS THIS CRYSTAL FROM?**
Dealers should know the provenance of their crystals, which includes country of origin. Sadly, when you buy a crystal, it will probably have gone through a long chain of handlers, so the actual mine may be hard to track down.

✴ **DO YOU CLEANSE YOUR CRYSTALS?**
It's good to buy crystals from someone who cleanses them. For one thing, it shows that the seller cares about them, which is a very important factor. Again, you will come to see the crystals' energy and feel this for yourself. However, I advise you to cleanse your crystals as soon as you buy them, no matter if the seller has done so or not, because it's a very good habit to get into.

✴ **HOW HAVE THE CRYSTALS BEEN PACKAGED?**
The reality is that a lot of crystals are wrapped in newspaper and flung into big metal crates. I saw this at the first crystals show I went to in America and it did upset me. The way a crystal is packaged impacts it. I display my crystals in a cabinet or in clean, compartmented storage boxes, wrapped in tissue paper, before I sell them. There's something about using newspaper that makes me feel sad. Crystals deserve to be wrapped in something much softer.

Crystal tool kit

There are so many crystals on the market and new ones are being found all the time, with new energetic frequencies to work with. I have a number of crystals that I feel are great for a beginner and these are the main ones I work with in this book; descriptions can be found between pages 24 and 30. They are:

* CLEAR QUARTZ
* SELENITE
* ROSE QUARTZ
* AMETHYST

* SMOKY QUARTZ
* CITRINE
* SHUNGITE

Later in the book, in Time to Tune In (page 52), I go into detail about the connection between crystals and the chakras, an ancient Indian system of energy centres located all around the body, with the seven key ones illustrated opposite. It is thought that the energy in crystals interacts with the energy in and around our bodies, and certain crystals resonate well with specific chakra points, for energetic healing. For example, amethyst, which is purple, can provide healing for the third eye chakra, bringing clarity, intuition and calm focus.

I have listed which chakras align with the crystals in my recommended tool kit so that you can begin to explore this connection between crystals and the chakras. You can simply place the crystals on the corresponding chakra and it will begin working with your energy, bringing you back into balance.

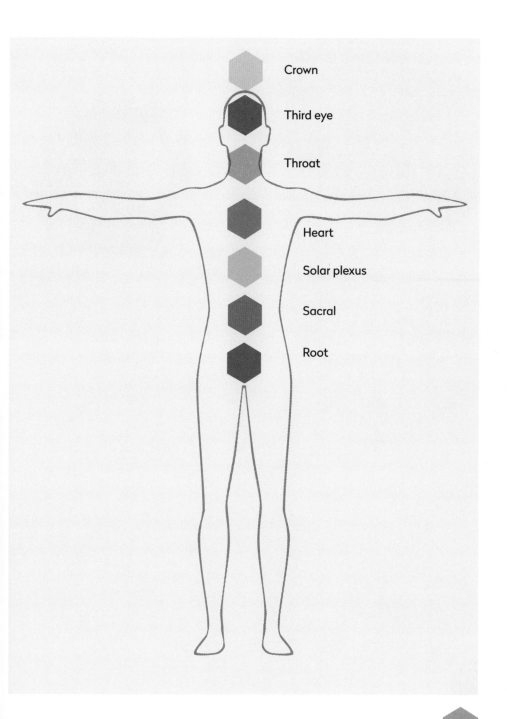

Crown

Third eye

Throat

Heart

Solar plexus

Sacral

Root

Amethyst

Shungite

Selenite

Citrine

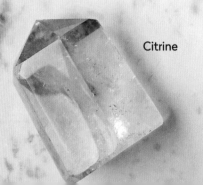

Smoky quartz

Rose quartz

Clear quartz

CLEAR QUARTZ

Chakra alignment: all, especially crown, third eye

✳ This is my master healer tool, a source of divine healing light and a crystal for expansion, amplifying and cleansing. I use it for everything and pair it with absolutely all my crystals – it gives them a boost and amplifies their energy. If you have just one crystal in your tool box, make it this one, a clear quartz crystal point. It holds within it all seven of the colour rays that affect the chakra systems, so it works on aligning all of your chakras at once to re-balance you.

✳ Clear quartz opens your higher chakras, especially your crown, to let in more light to circulate around your body. It clears hazy and blocked energy through all layers of your aura, especially around your crown, giving you clarity of mind, helping you to focus and be more conscious and in the present.

✳ It expands your aura, opening your heart and mind to higher guidance and enhancing communication with crystals, plants and animals, and is especially helpful in connecting you to your higher self. An excellent channelling crystal for journaling and spiritual development.

✳ As a good crystal to have with you when manifesting and strengthening positive affirmations, it has the ability to focus, intensify, record and transform energy. It was one of the great record-keeper crystals used in Atlantis and Lemurian times (page 143).

SELENITE

Chakra alignment: crown, third eye

✳ Selenite opens up and expands the crown chakra, making it a great tool for inner wisdom, psychic development, journeying, refreshing and collecting more life-force energy into your body. Every time I have guided people to work with selenite at their crown their visions have become clearer, their state of relaxation goes deeper and they trust their intuition even more.

✳ Selenite imparts a soft, gentle, mothering energy deeply connected to the moon. It also aids contact with the angels, bringing you their protection.

✳ Brilliant for cleansing and protecting your space, selenite brings pure refreshing light to your aura and room.

✳ It removes energy blocks from the physical and etheric bodies, and also from other crystals.

✳ A good protector during childbirth and throughout motherhood, it also promotes fertility.

✳ The crystal of love, selenite helps you to maintain a loving relationship with yourself and those around you.

✳ Since it opens your crown chakra, if you are especially sensitive, be careful where you put it. Your bedside table might not be the best place unless you want wonderful astral adventures (page 148). I have had many a session with people suddenly having trouble sleeping, and I knew full well they had selenite by the bed or under the pillow.

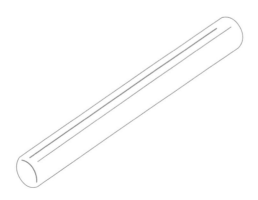

ROSE QUARTZ

Chakra alignment: heart

✳ This crystal opens you up to love in all its forms and is my number-one ally in helping me to love myself a little more. It's the crystal of unconditional love, teaching you to honour yourself, see your worth and know that you are worthy, believe in yourself, love the very bones of you and just be open to love in all its forms.

✳ Rose quartz is heart activating – it keeps your heart open, protecting you but also making sure you don't build up any protective walls. If you have erected any walls or barriers around your heart, it will gently help you to take them down, enabling you to see the bigger picture in a loving way. It teaches you how to forgive yourself and others, and how to be compassionate to all involved in any situation.

✳ Rose quartz's soft, gentle energy will come over you in nurturing waves. Try visualizing these as pink rays washing over you from head to toe. Take a moment to pause and breathe in that loving light while holding the crystal.

✳ Rose quartz is very good at relaxing you and aiding deep sleep – no nightmares here! – so place your crystal by your bedside or under your pillow.

✳ This crystal lowers stress, balances your energy and gives confidence.

✳ A brilliant crystal to hold when reading positive affirmations, or on your heart while meditating, rose quartz's structure and energetic nature mean it holds affirmations really well, working on supporting you with them through love.

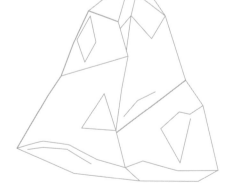

AMETHYST

Chakra alignment: crown, third eye

✳ A calming crystal, good to meditate with, amethyst has high vibrations, which means it can enhance psychic connection and development since it can work to the higher chakras. This also means it may not make a good bedside companion.

✳ Very much a focus crystal, once it has worked on calming your mind and absorbing worries it becomes the ideal tool for decision making. It supports success in business, attracting wealth, and helps your path become clear so you can always move forward in life.

✳ Amethyst magnifies the energy of other crystals and offers good all-round gentle protection. It's great to have in your pocket or bag when you are out, to protect you against negativity. When

I hold my amethyst at the end of the day, it is warm – a sign that it's been busy doing its job and absorbing.

✳ It can balance all levels of your auric field, your emotional, mental and physical body.

✳ Working on the emotional body, amethyst can help to combat obsessive thinking, and calms any anger you might hold, as well as grief and nerves.

✳ An energy enhancer, amethyst boosts your self-esteem.

✳ Physically, it is good for hormone balance, detoxing, hearing, insomnia, viral infections, the bones, heart and stomach. It was known by the ancient Greeks as a "sober" crystal because it helped ease hangovers and addiction.

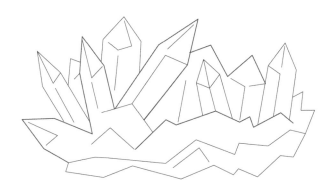

SMOKY QUARTZ

Chakra alignment: root

✳ Smoky quartz is a very protective crystal. I mostly use it to absorb any negativity around me; worries or anxieties seem to float away when I hold smoky quartz. It transmutes them into something positive that your body can recycle.

✳ Due to its gentle, grounding energy, it helps you to re-balance, detoxify and release past hurt.

✳ Its vibrations are earthy – a good crystal to help you raise your own vibrations during any energy work.

✳ Ask it to absorb any lower vibrations you have picked up during the day and place it at the side of the bed.

✳ Smoky quartz works on the kidneys and other organs to eliminate toxins. It also restores vigour and shines a light on any gifts that you may be hiding in the shadows of your soul.

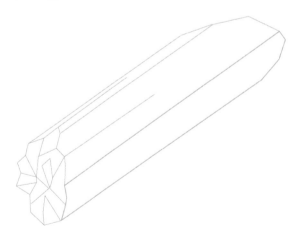

CITRINE

Chakra alignment: solar plexus

✳ Natural citrine is a great manifester crystal – a crystal that has the ability to bring the right energies to you, to help manifest or create that which you desire in your life.

✳ A glorious warm sunshine energy that refreshes, re-energizes and gives you a boost accompanies citrine. It brings new beginnings and fresh opportunities into your life, attracting love and happiness.

✳ It stimulates the brain, aiding concentration and awakening creativity and imagination. Citrine has the power to transmute negative into positive, helping you to see negative patterns around you and bring them to the light.

✳ Known as the merchant's crystal for its ability to bring wealth and success, citrine in your purse may help to attract money to you.

✳ Citrine brings pure joy to your heart and its yellow and gold rays work on your solar plexus and navel to remove any blocks.

✳ Good for those who are highly sensitive or empathetic, because it increases the amount of protective light around the body and also keeps vibrations high.

✳ Physically, citrine supports the endocrine and digestive systems and relieves menstrual or menopausal symptoms.

SHUNGITE

Chakra alignment: root

✳ A crystal that intrigues me, shungite is more mineral than crystal; some say that one day it will be valued as highly as gold. Recently I am seeing it everywhere, which is a telltale sign that as a collective consciousness we need its protective energy.

✳ For me, it's a master protector, a grounding, strong, ancient healer, from Russia. When I hold it, I feel an impenetrable shield of black surrounding me, which allows only positive and useful energies to reach my aura.

✳ It purifies and detoxifies the body. Made of almost pure carbon, it's one of the only natural minerals to contain fullerenes (particular carbon molecules), which may have antioxidant properties and be of potential use in the treatment of cancer. Shungite is therefore attracting plenty of interest as the subject of research.

✳ It shields you from all electromagnetic frequencies and geopathic stress, all forms of negative energy around you, transmuting it into something positive that the body can use. It may even protect you from bacteria.

✳ Clean it and add it to water to make high-vibrational protective water to drink. I find its vibration gentle enough for sensitive people.

✳ Hold it to your heart and say, "I am protected, I am safe," and it will hold that intention for you.

✳ Shungite placed by electrical equipment, phones, computers and TVs will block those rays from reaching you.

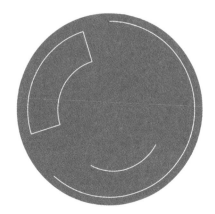

How to keep and store crystals

It's always wonderful to keep your crystals on show, but if you do, remember to cleanse them (page 32), as they will absorb a lot of other people's energy. Crystals go through restful periods but they activate as soon as you show them attention and focus. When transporting them, it's good to keep them in a small pouch made of natural fibres to protect them from other energies but also from damage.

Some people prefer to pack their crystals away when not in use, and this is valid too. Anyone who has a lot of crystals and uses them for healing might want to keep certain ones stored. Just use your intuition on where to put them. It's sensible not to place them in areas of intense vibration, for example on top of electrical equipment, because they absorb those frequencies. The exception is shungite, or any other protecting crystal, which actually blocks these vibrations before they reach your energy field. Crystals that improve concentration and focus, such as amethyst and citrine, are helpful in the work place.

I prefer to keep my crystals out on show where I can shower them with love – this keeps them dust free and singing as well as helping their energy flow to remain regular. For example, it's best to face a crystal point toward the magnetic flow of the earth – so turn the point of the crystal toward magnetic south and the base toward north. This is not essential, but if you do have the chance to try it, please do and see what differences you detect.

Cleansing and energizing crystals

Crystals need and love to be both cleansed of old energy and charged, or energized, with new. In this section you will discover some ways you can do this at home. For example, if you happen to put a crystal on the lawn overnight, it will be both cleansed by the dew and energized by the moonlight!

Why cleanse?

This always seems to be the first question I'm asked and I think a lot of people get hung up on the cleansing part – it's not as long-winded as it sounds and can take moments. So why do you cleanse crystals? Because they have been handled by many people before they get to you and they may have been mistreated or misused or come from a negative environment. So it's good to cleanse them as soon as you get them, but it's also important to trust that your crystals are actually highly efficient at maintaining their energy flow and balance.

HOW OFTEN SHOULD I CLEANSE A CRYSTAL?

✳ Whenever it looks dusty or sticky – cleanse a crystal when you think it needs it.

✳ Before and after you have worked with it.

✳ If someone else has handled it.

✳ If you have gone through a big change in your life.

✳ If you want to use it in a ritual or ceremony.

Cleansing rituals

Over the next few pages I have outlined the ways in which crystals can be cleansed. However, before cleansing I would advise you to check online, or with the seller direct, if a new crystal you have bought or received can be damaged by water, salt or sunlight.

✳ WATER: A clean source of fresh water is best but if you do not have that close by, distilled or tap water will suffice. I often hold crystals under running water and hear them sigh a happy sigh, an "oh gosh, I really needed that" sigh. I imagine it's like that feeling when you get into a warm shower or bath and your muscles and body just relax; it really feels like that kind of release for me. Occasionally, crystals gather dust and negative energy and just need a wash. You might want to throw a little salt into the water – I do this to bathe and cleanse my hands after a healing session. However, some crystals do not like water:

– Selenite and other forms of gypsum
– Mica
– Angelite
– Celestite
– Calcite
– Lepidolite
– Tourmaline
– Pearls
– Opal
– Raw malachite
– Turquoise
– Forms of rock salt including halite

✳ OTHER CRYSTALS: Some crystals are self-cleansing and they cleanse other crystals around them as well. Great examples of this are selenite, kyanite (all colours), natural citrine, carnelian and azeztulite.

Quartz or amethyst crystal caves, beds or clusters can be used to absorb negative energy from crystals, but also to re-infuse them with positive energy. Place the crystals within the cave or on the bed or cluster and leave them for a couple of days or for as long as you feel they need.

✳ SMUDGING: Native Americans traditionally use white sage, which absorbs negative energy, and sweet grass, which brings positivity to the energy field of whatever it is you are cleansing – yourself, your crystals, your space. You can use sandalwood, cedarwood or palo santo wood in the same way. Tie a bunch into what's called a smudge stick, light the end, blow out the flame and let the smoke pass over the crystal – if the smoke comes into contact with the space around the crystal, it's enough; passing the crystal through the smoke is good, too. Traditionally, a feather is used to fan the smoke around, but I blow it to where it needs to go. You might want to utter an intention while doing this – something like: "I wish to take any negative energy out of this crystal and transmute it to only good positive energy" – to strengthen the process.

✳ SOUND: You could chant to your crystals or even sing happy songs to them – no heavy metal, please. Playing singing bowls and chimes cleanses the crystals' vibrations and your space at the same time.

✳ AURA SPRAYS: You can buy premixed protection sprays to spritz over your crystals – just make sure the crystals are not among those that don't like being exposed to liquids (see "water", page 33).

✳ SALT OR RICE: Either will absorb any negativity the crystals have accumulated. Immerse them in a bowl of Himalayan salt, or rice, overnight or for up to a week, and always run them under the tap afterward to rinse away any residue.

Since you then have to throw away the salt or rice, I find this method a bit wasteful, and if you have a lot of crystals, as I do, it would have to be a pretty big bowl of salt! Some people place the crystals in a glass container and bury that in the salt, but again you have to throw it all away. Crystals that are porous, have a high metal content or contain water, for example pyrite, opal, hematite, malachite or lapis lazuli, should not be cleansed in this way.

✳ THE EARTH: Planting crystals back into the earth really restores them; grounding and protecting crystals love this because it wipes them clean and nourishes them. Bury them in a plant pot – keep it indoors – for anything from one to a few days, depending on how deeply you feel they need cleansing.

CLEANSING VISUALIZATION

This is my favourite way to cleanse crystals – visualization with healing light. Anyone can do it, it's so simple, and the more you practise it, the quicker it becomes. You have to think on it for just a moment and it's done.

✳ Hold the crystal to your heart and take three long, deep breaths to centre yourself. Then begin to lengthen each breath so you are holding the breath in for as long as you are breathing it out.

✳ Start to breathe each breath into your heart, with the intention to open it. Each inhale is expanding and opening up your heart, at the front and at the back. You may like to visualize a pink rose where your heart is and see each petal opening with every exhale.

✳ Start to see and feel a beam of light from your heart reaching out in front of you. It could be white or golden – go with what you feel.

✳ The cord of light will travel straight to the centre of the crystal, lighting it up from the inside. Expand that golden glow within the crystal and push anything negative out of it. Spin that light round if it helps you to visualize flinging out negative spots or dense energy. Soon the crystal becomes glowing and refreshed.

✳ All the while you are holding the crystal with the intention to cleanse it. Don't doubt it. Then thank the crystal when you feel it is done; it might even thank you back!

Energizing crystals

Native Americans believe that crystals naturally energize themselves from our body's energy field, and physical contact does give your crystals a boost. So pick them up, hold them and rub them between your hands as often as you can.

Crystals also love to be out in the elements, rain or shine, and in contact with the earth. They resonate with nature and this is the best way to re-energize them.

✳ MOONLIGHT: Lunar energy is very gentle and nurturing and the light of the full moon is great for cleansing and re-energizing your crystals. Selenite in particular is linked to the moon – named after the moon goddess Selene – and loves a good moon bath to re-energize. Anything clear or white will really resonate with the moon's energy.

I'm often asked, "If I don't put my crystals out in direct moonlight, will it still work?" The answer is absolutely yes. Put them on a window ledge where they can bask in the moon's rays, if that's convenient.

Why? Because energy knows no bounds; it has no limitations. According to quantum physics it has no time or space restraints. Just because there's a window in the way does not mean the crystals will not feel the lunar energy – and not only on the night of the full moon but also the days before and after.

✳ SUNSHINE: The natural energy transmitted by the sun can energize your crystals. Leave them out, from an hour to a day, but remember that the sun's rays are powerful and some crystals fade when left out in strong sunlight for any length of time. Early morning or late afternoon is best for them. Amethyst and heat-treated citrine, for example, should not be left out in the sun for long. The same applies to placing them on a window ledge.

Programming a crystal

Crystals can do so much, it's always good to ask them to do something for you, whether it's holding it to your heart and surrounding it with your light, wishing for it to work to your "highest good" – this is giving the crystal permission to send the energy where it needs to go. Or you might have a specific wish in mind. For example, if you are working with rose quartz around inner issues of self-love, you could say the following: "I program this crystal to help me accept the right love in all of its forms."

Always be clear and state your intent by starting with "I wish to program this crystal to ..."

Holding that intent for a few moments while you surround the crystal in your heart's light is enough, or hold it for however long you feel it needs.

Choosing a crystal

You don't have to think too deeply about selecting a crystal. Sometimes you can be drawn to its colour – the perfect tint of lilac or the coolest shade of neon (hello, Mr Sulfur!) that would look amazing on your bedside table. You are attracted to it and that's what counts. When you looked at it, it made you smile and stirred something in you.

If you go to a crystal store and find yourself picking one up and holding it without much thought, you have already made your choice. In holding it you have made your connection to it, started working with it.

You might need that gentle, lilac, heart-warming glow and not even realize it, but your energy field does, subtly. You might have reached for the neon-yellow mineral because you have some underlying emotional issues that need release – yellow is the colour of your solar plexus chakra, your emotional centre – or you might need a confidence boost. People can become too tangled up with the "why" and forget that working with a crystal is about feeling; it goes beyond the mind.

QUARTZ

Our planet is built on quartz – beautiful and strong and the most abundant crystal, it keeps the energy and magnetic grids of this world we live in balanced. Quartz is always a good place to start when looking for a crystal. It comes in many different shades, depending on its mineral content and the temperature it was warmed to in the earth. You have rose quartz, with that delicious pale pink loving glow; smoky quartz, still translucent but earthy and brown; and amethyst, the most beautiful violet shade that calms and connects.

Crystal gifts

When a friend gifts you a crystal, take note because it always carries a special message. Your friend could be a silent messenger, passing it on, or maybe he or she used intuition to bring you something you need. The gift is no accident. The crystals you need will find a way of getting to you.

I have a friend who was given three pieces of selenite by three different people one Christmas. She didn't need to know the exact properties of selenite to hear the message loud and clear. She just needed selenite's energy near her to support her at that time.

CONNECTING TO A CRYSTAL ONLINE

If you can't get to a crystal store, you can still form a connection with a crystal that you see online without it being physically with you. Recently a dear friend read one of my blog posts about danburite and messaged me straightaway to say that she could not get past the third paragraph because her whole arm went numb. She just could not move her hand and had to stop reading. Why was that? I told her it was a very strong sign that she needed danburite's energy in her life – she resonated with its energy through my words and the photographs.

"I am connected to the universal life flow of the universe, I am open to its energy, its flow, it is within me and all around me, we are one and the same."

If a crystal breaks

Sometimes a careless accident results in damage. I can't tell you the number of times a crystal has fallen out of my pocket and cracked on my tiled bathroom floor. Every time, it hurts me and makes me sad because I feel I have mistreated it. I instantly scoop it up and say sorry, and either keep it or bury it in the earth.

The energy of that crystal is not affected in any way; it's still there. Think of the huge pieces of quartz that are mined from the earth and mostly broken down into smaller pieces to sell.

Most of the time, when a crystal breaks in two, it is a message that only you may be able to feel intuitively. Maybe someone close to you needs that energy, too, and that piece is for him or her. Sometimes if a crystal breaks or disappears, it's because it has done its work with you.

I once had a prized piece of phantom quartz. It wasn't the most expensive crystal but it turned out to be one of my biggest teachers. It travelled with me everywhere. I used it to channel spirit and I felt I could channel so clearly just because of the crystal. Whenever I did readings, it sat with me and I held it, believing it was the key to my writing so much from spirit. I thought that I *needed* it. One day it broke in two for no reason. I had not dropped it, it just collapsed, and I cried. Man, I cried so hard. I asked why this had happened and I heard very clearly, "You do not need that crystal. You are the channel." So this was my lesson, teaching me not to place too much importance on something external when all I need is within. Many messages can come with a broken crystal; we just have to be open to receiving them.

MISSING CRYSTALS

I have had mysterious instances of crystals disappearing when I was absolutely certain where I had placed them. They have a way of disappearing when they have finished their work with you, or if theirs is not an appropriate energy for you at that time. Instead of being sad that a crystal has gone, it is good to smile and thank it for its healing and the lessons it brought you.

Every crystal has a story

Each crystal comes to you for a reason and I find that listening to other people's stories is the most beautiful way to learn.

As well as sharing with you my own story on the next page, I've asked a few women with whom I've worked to share theirs. They have truly delved into the depths of their heart to tell of one crystal that has had a particular impact on their journey. It might be the first crystal they bought or the one that has resonated the most. Each story is different and the way each person perceives and feels energy is different. In sharing their stories, you may gain some clarity and resonance of your own.
I have learned as I work with crystals and crystalline sound that there is great beauty in listening, truly listening, with your inner ear to the magic that others can hold and share.

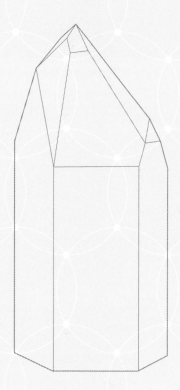

MY STORY

The first crystal I came by was not a crystal at all but a rather dusty, rubbly, holey rock from the garden. My cousin told me that it was moon rock from an asteroid that had hit our garden hundreds of years ago. I was seven. I believed this and thought that rock was the most magical thing I owned. I slept with it every night under my pillow. I loved the possibility that it had come from another world, from space, and imagined all the things it had seen. Looking back, I really believe that the amount of love I gave that dusty rock lifted its vibrations. It made me happy when I held it. It helped ground my fly-away energy.

Everything living has an energy field, and a rock or pebble is no different, even though it may not be as pretty as rose quartz. Shamans use flint as a talisman and grounding tool in their journeying and vision-quest ceremonies, and raw flint is a big chunk of brown rock. I often collect four pebbles from the garden and use them to grid and cleanse a room, placing one in each corner and asking that they remove the room's negativity. After a few days I wash them and take them far away from my house.

So my story is humble. A simple little fake moon rock sparked my journey and love of natural minerals and crystals.

"The feeling you get when you fall in love with a crystal is the best feeling; it lights you up from the inside."

A GREEN JASPER TALISMAN

Stephanie Victoire, writer and creator of Petal and Moss Apothecary.

When I found my first crystal necklace in a shop in Glastonbury some years ago, I knew that I was beginning a new and powerful journey with crystal energy. This particular piece of jasper was a beautiful oval shape in a gorgeous shade of forest green. But what drew me to it so strongly were its markings, which happened to be in the shape of a powerful, old tree, speaking to me of wisdom and growth. I immediately knew this pendant was for me. I wore it every day from then on for approximately two years. I found myself tending to it every morning before looping it around my neck and wearing it at my throat chakra, almost like a choker. I developed sensitivity to it, intuitively knowing how to cleanse it and activate it. Each morning, before leaving the house, I would hold the pendant and "pull" stagnant energy from it, imagining black or grey threads being extracted from the crystal. I would "drop" these threads into an imaginary bowl of pure white light, then bathe the whole pendant in this light, before placing it to my heart and saying the words, "I program this crystal to operate for my highest good today, keeping me clear, aligned and grounded."

Everyday contact with this green jasper meant that my physical body was being altered because my energetic body was being raised. With this attunement to higher vibration, I was able to feel tingles in my hands whenever I picked up a happy, healthy crystal that wanted to come home with me. I encountered many interactions while wearing my jasper for all to see. Colleagues at work who were usually conservative in their thinking or unsure of spirituality would engage in esoteric conversations with me. They would start wearing bright colours to work, read empowering books during their lunch break, bring new plants in for their desks and become more creative.

I was living in my truth by wearing a crystal talisman at my throat, and this encouraged others to live in their truth, too – the power of growth and wisdom. The last time I wore that jasper was the day before I set off on a solo trip around the world. I didn't want to lose it, but in a great way, we had already achieved our work together.

ANGELIC HEALER

Rhiannon Bradley's connection with angelite, the crystal that supported and held her through her journeys with cancer.

I have always felt an affinity with crystals, even as a young child, and that feeling has become stronger as the years have gone by. As a teenager I had a trusty amethyst and a calming moon crystal that I carried around with me, not really knowing why but knowing I wanted them near me. I began to connect strongly with crystals after my first battle with cancer, when I became a reiki healer.

I was diagnosed with thyroid cancer at the age of 24 and, a year after my treatment, my reiki master taught me about crystals and how to use them to aid the healing process. One crystal that she gifted me was a perfectly spherical piece of angelite. It reminded me of a little planet and I instantly felt there was something otherworldly about it. I feel drawn to it for many reasons. On a physical level, it helps to balance and heal my throat chakra, as I have had organs removed and a major physical trauma there. I have found myself reaching for it when I have needed some celestial guidance. I mostly placed it on my throat, letting it fall nicely into the dip of my neck. Its colour came through vibrationally, its energy a gently swirling planetary feeling like Venus.

I needed its strength and guidance during my breast cancer diagnosis at the age of 32 and once again found myself connecting deeply with my angelite. I meditated with it every day to help strengthen my connection with my guides and angels. I could feel its deep comfort and dedication to keeping me in tune with my higher self even with my foggy chemobrain. It tells me that there is "more than meets the eye" and encourages me to have faith in myself and the timing of my life. I don't need to know the answer to everything; a little mystery can be a good thing. It has helped me open up to acceptance and forgiveness and come out on the other side of two cancers without anger or regret, knowing that these experiences have made me more receptive spiritually and provided incredible opportunities, for which I am eternally grateful.

A BEAUTIFUL CONNECTION
TO CRYSTALS

Mary Warren and her family received a deeper love for their crystals.

My family fell in love with crystals the moment we truly invited them into our lives. I was looking for healing and connection for myself. What we ended up with was much more than we could have expected. My children, especially my youngest boy, had an automatic connection. The school year was turning out to be quite tough for him and we really looked to the power of the crystals to aid him. Every morning he would scoop up two or three or ten crystals for his pockets and he started to feel braver, less scared, more grounded and steady. He stopped telling the world he hated school. He started seeing his own potential. His self-confidence changed from nothing to abundant. It all started with him being dazzled by my crystals that would arrive in the mail; he now has a collection almost lovelier than mine. Most of all, he loves school now. He stands tall and full of pride.

PAST-LIFE REMEMBRANCE

Emma Mulholland's connection to her Master Quartz has given her a great deal of clarity.

My beloved Master Quartz came into my life about 15 years ago, a beautiful clear quartz with many markings, lines and a strong divine masculine presence. He was gifted to me by a dear soul whom I used to visit regularly for reiki healing and my practitioner-level training. He communicated to me that his preferred name was "Master Quartz" only a few months ago. It has taken me this long to work with him because I feel I was not ready for this level of connection.

I meditated with him and was taken to a past life in the Americas as a young shaman who was persecuted for spying on the elders in the tribe (I was thirsty for their secrets!). I clutched my quartz during the vision and he was glowing in my mind's eye throughout, delighted that I had finally tapped into his power. He then told me that he has been with me in many lifetimes, which was extraordinarily moving. As a legal professional I deal in logic for most of my waking life, but I have realized that logic is just a small proportion of what it means to be part of human existence and these gems given to us by Mother Earth are wise beyond words.

PART 2

Time to Tune In

It's all energy

The sooner you become aware of your own energy and the energies around you, the sooner seeing and feeling crystal energy will flow. This goes hand in hand with discovery of the self. Everything living has an energy field. You can connect with the energy of plants and trees, places, the earth you stand on, the air you breathe. In this chapter, I have included some exercises to help you open up your intuition and awareness of energy.

Once you have acquired a new crystal I want you simply to sit with it and gaze at it. Examine every nook and cranny with your eyes, inviting in its energy to you as you hold it. This is all I do. I get into my

sacred space, calm my mind and go within and listen. I have a series of questions I ask the crystal and myself once I am calm and feeling from my heart space.

Talk to your crystals. You may feel crazy at first, but you will notice a boost in their energy. They will shine more, they will just look happier, their energy will lift and the more you are around this energy, the more you will sense the changes. Another wonderful practice is to thank them after you have worked with them. They love this, because who doesn't love being appreciated?

WHICH HAND DO I USE WHEN HOLDING A CRYSTAL?

I'm trying to refrain from posing the questions back to you, but ask yourself which hand you want to use. The key is to ask ourselves these questions and listen to the first intuitive answer.

The truth is it's up to you. The left side of your body is known as the receiving side, your feminine side, and a lot of people advise you to use the left hand to receive crystal energy. Your right side is your masculine, giving side, so hold the crystal in your right hand when connecting with it and programming it. But if you want to hold your rose quartz in your right hand, there's a reason for that, so do it.

WAYS WE PERCEIVE ENERGY

You can perceive energy in many different ways and these are not exclusive. The more you develop and the more you practise, the more of these senses you open up. Identifying how you perceive energy will help you understand how your energy field interacts with other energy.

✳ CLAIRVOYANCE / *"clear sight"*
The gift of seeing past, present and future in your mind's eye – or third eye. Receiving symbols and visions beyond the limitations of time or space.

✳ CLAIRAUDIENCE / *"clear hearing"*
The ability to perceive sounds or words through your inner ear. Many mediums like myself work with both clairvoyance and clairaudience.

✳ CLAIRSENTIENCE / *"clear feeling"*
The gift of perceiving information through a strong "feeling" throughout your body. That gut reaction, just feeling something to your core, that's clairsentience.

✳ CLAIRSCENT / *"clear smelling"*
The gift of smelling odours or food that are not in your surroundings and not perceived through the physical nose, but that are beyond any limitations of time and space. For example, when working with spirits I have often had instances when I have smelt their aftershave or strong tobacco smoke, if they were a smoker.

✳ CLAIRTANGENCY / *"clear touch"*
Also known as psychometry, this is the gift of being able to touch an object or place and knowing its history through information received.

✳ CLAIRGUSTANCE / *"clear taste"*
Being able to taste a substance before putting it into your mouth. Being able to perceive the essence of something through the spirit realm.

✳ CLAIREMPATHY / *"clear emotion"*
Being able to tune into someone else's emotional experience, whether it's a person, animal or place.

Grounding

Grounding is the first thing I learned how to do when I began working with energy. It has become an important part of my rituals when meditating and working with others. I recommend making a grounding practice part of your daily morning routine: it is important to ground yourself before working with crystals.

Grounding means establishing a connection to the earth by bringing your energy down and anchoring it. It also works a treat for those fly-away moments when you need more focus, you feel light-headed, dizzy, not really present, and if you are worried or anxious.

CREATING A GROUNDING CORD

There are a number of ways to ground yourself (see box opposite) but my favourite is to create a grounding cord. Once it is in place you can always check in with it, repair it or cut it and create a new one.

* First take a few breaths to centre yourself, making each inhale deeper than the last. Feel your body, muscles and cells relax and open. Imagine breathing in white light and breathe out any anxieties or worries.

* Once in a relaxed state, draw your focus to your root chakra (page 60), see a ball of spinning green light there, hold it and feel it spin. You are in control of this powerful orb of light and when you are ready to let it go, release it.

* See it tunnel down into the earth, through layer and layer, deeper down, through the crystalline layers, until it reaches the core of the earth.

* Now it forms a long tunnel, a cord of green light connecting you to the earth's core. Flex the cord and feel the connection.

* On your next inhale, feel yourself pulling up earth energy through this cord and into your root chakra. Take it up through each chakra in turn. Feel it filling you up, feel your connection to the earth and how you are held and loved.

You have now established your cord. Check on it from time to time to see that it is still intact, patch it up with white light if it feels weak, or cut it and start the exercise again.

WAYS TO GROUND YOURSELF

As well as creating a grounding cord (see opposite), you can also ground yourself physically.

✳ Hold a grounding crystal. Black, brown or red crystals tend to be grounding. My favourites are black tourmaline, shungite, smoky quartz, black obsidian, red jasper, moss agate, tourmalated quartz, aragonite, petrified wood, unakite and black moon crystal.

✳ Use earthy aromatherapy oils, such as cedarwood, pine, sandalwood or frankincense.

✳ Stand with your bare feet on the ground.

✳ Go for a walk and connect with nature, listen to the birds or the wind in the trees.

✳ Drink some water.

✳ Eat some root vegetables.

You can also use visualization.

✳ Imagine that you are wearing concrete blocks on your feet, or moon boots while listening to Sting playing *Walking on the Moon*. This will hold your energy down.

✳ Plant your feet on the ground and imagine roots growing from the soles of your feet down through the soil below you, holding you.

Attuning to a crystal

Attuning is just a fancy word for "connecting". Life is full of connections; it's built on connections – to ourself, our loved ones, the earth, our spirit, the elements ... All of these connections are integral to us; they shape us and help us grow.

The most important thing you can do is to build a connection to the crystal you have chosen to work with. It's a give-and-take relationship – the more you put in, the more benefits you receive. You forged this connection when you first held it. If you don't work with a crystal much, forget to cleanse and refresh it, its energy dulls down and it goes into a restful state. This living thing will respond well to attention in the form of love, so send it love. Send it sunshine and happy thoughts, praise it, sing to it – whatever feels right to you.

CONNECT WITH YOUR CRYSTAL

✶ Select a crystal you feel drawn to, or ask your crystals which one to choose – you will feel one wanting to be chosen.

✶ Take time to sit or lie down in a space where you feel comfortable with no distractions. The steps you take to be calm are as important as the process of connecting – the moments spent focusing your thoughts or the pauses between deep breaths.

✶ Create stillness in your core, breathe and hold the crystal in your left hand.

✶ Bring the crystal to your heart with intention to connect with it on a deep level.

✶ See a beautiful cord of golden light reaching out from your heart and connecting with the crystal you are holding. It goes through and into the core of the crystal and lights it up from the inside.

✶ In that moment you have forged a deep connection. Of course, the intention to connect is enough, but all of these visuals and energetic cords help to strengthen the connection and build on it.

✶ Thank your crystal for stepping up to help you and hold it with a grateful heart.

✶ Open your heart to receive and write down any feelings that come to you during or after doing this exercise to help you understand what healing work you could be doing on yourself.

"I am connected to
the earth and her wisdom,
her knowledge and power flow up
through me, I am safe, I am protected,
I am held.

I let go of any energy that does not
serve my highest good,

I am grounded and my root
chakra is balanced."

Chakras and crystalline energy

Chakras are a system of energy centres in and around the body. There are actually 114 in the body, but we tend to be familiar with the seven main ones – root, sacral, solar plexus, heart, throat, third eye, crown.

The chakras regulate the flow of "prana" or life-force energy around us. When one or more of these chakras is blocked or the energy is not flowing as efficiently as it could, physical illness may result. If we do not express ourselves outwardly, then things can manifest inwardly, causing a blockage, so it's good to become aware of these energy centres and use crystals to re-balance and release them.

Crystals of a certain colour or vibration work with certain chakras. You can re-balance your body by placing a suitable crystal on the relevant chakra, laying them on from crown to root, all the way down and leaving them there for as long as you feel you need to, holding the intention to re-balance and release. Though the colours of my crystal choices on the opposite page vary slightly from the chakra colours identified on page 21 you will know that, as an intuitive healer, I believe crystals' identities aren't static. I encourage you to chose the crystals to which you feel lead as I do, and have done, in selecting both these and the crystals in my toolkit guide (page 20). The heart chakra can be a little confusing because the colour generally associated with it is green. It has pink as a second colour, hence the rose quartz working so well with the energy of the heart chakra.

Opening the chakras

The more open you are energetically, the deeper crystals can support you, and having your chakras open is important. The intention of wanting to open your chakras will open them, but I like to support that with a visualization. Remember that they open at the front and back.

Crown chakra — Clear quartz

Third eye chakra — Labradorite

Throat chakra — Angelite

Heart chakra — Rose quartz

Solar plexus chakra — Golden healer quartz

Sacral chakra — Carnelian

Root chakra — Red jasper

OPENING YOUR CHAKRAS WITH WHITE LIGHT

Select the crystals that wish to support you and place them on and around you. You can use a full chakra set or just select a couple that you intuitively place on your body.

✳ Sit or lie in a quiet space where you feel relaxed.

✳ Take long, deep breaths to the bottom of your belly to ground yourself and centre your core.

✳ Bring your awareness to your crown, visualizing a closed white lotus flower on top of your head. Notice a beam of brilliant white light extending down from the cosmos to the top of the lotus flower. Feel its intense, warm, loving glow.

✳ Start to open the petals of this flower one by one. When it is fully open, feel the white light cascade down into your crown, filling it up, expanding it, opening it and pushing out anything that does not belong there.

✳ When you feel ready, pull the light down to your third eye, where it pools, washing around and expanding and opening that chakra until you see indigo light beaming out, front and back.

✳ Next take this white light down to your throat, your blue energy centre.

Again, it expands and opens your throat chakra to beam out brilliant blue light, front and back.

✳ Take the column of white light down to your heart, creating space for it to wash through and open your heart, beaming out green light, front and back.

✳ Next bring it down to your solar plexus, your yellow energy centre, expanding, opening, activating it, pushing out anything that does not serve you any more. See this brilliant sunshine energy beam out in front and behind you.

✳ Now the column of white light moves down to your sacral chakra, gently opening and expanding it, helping release what is ready to be released. You see orange light in front and behind you.

✳ The white-light column moves down to your root chakra, again expanding and opening it, strengthening your connection to the earth. You see red rays of light beaming out fully in front and behind you.

✳ Notice that this column of white light is going through all of your chakras, connecting and opening them fully from head to toe.

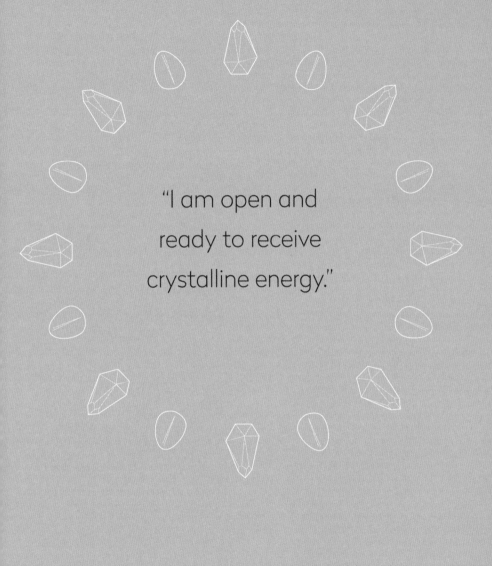

"I am open and
ready to receive
crystalline energy."

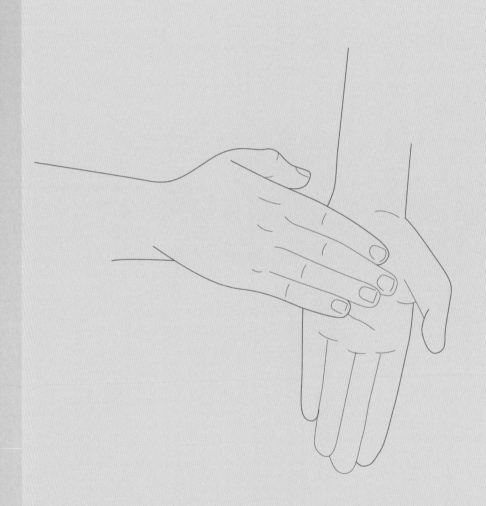

TIME TO TUNE IN

OPENING YOUR HAND CHAKRAS

If you experiment with holding a crystal before doing this and after you have finished, I promise you will feel an enormous difference. Hands are healing tools and opening their chakras will enable you to *feel* your crystals much more strongly.

✳ Hold out your left hand flat, palm facing up to the sky. Visualize orbs of light over your hand, including one large central one, which is your palm chakra.

✳ Keeping your left hand still, gaze at it and visualize your chakras. They appear on your palm and on your fingers. You may see them as closed flower buds or as balls of energy. Begin by swiping your right hand slowly across your left. From the palm down to the fingers, as you do this you will see these energy centres open, as if a blind has been pulled from them, so they beam out light. If you saw flowers you may see them in full bloom, radiating energy. Whatever the visual, hold the image of your hand chakras which are fully open beaming, light and energy.

You may find that your light is not white; it might be green, golden, blue or purple. This is your individual colour, which may change over time. If you do healing work with your hands, it can change depending on what energy you are channelling.

✳ Repeat this exercise again with your right hand.

FEELING YOUR ENERGY

Now that your hands are open we can have some fun with energy orbs.

✳ Hold your hands out at arm's length, palms facing, and slowly move them toward each other. Notice how you feel as your hands get closer. Is there some resistance? Can you feel the energy between your hands building? Let it take the shape of an orb between your hands.

✳ If you don't feel anything first time, repeat the process. Start by opening your hands again, as in the previous exercise, and then practise.

GETTING RID OF STUCK EMOTIONS

Once your hands are open and you have had some fun with creating energy orbs, I want you to get rid of any emotions, worries or anxieties you are holding from the day. Maybe you had an argument with someone, had a bad meeting or someone said something that has played on your mind for the rest of the day. It's time to let it go.

✳ Hold your hands close together, but with a big enough gap to visualize and feel an energy ball between them.

✳ Take a few calming blue breaths and centre yourself.

✳ When you feel ready, call up any emotions, memories or worries that are on your mind. Let them flow to the surface; don't question them. Ask yourself what emotions you are holding in your heart and why. Are they yours or someone else's?

✳ Push each one of them into the energy ball between your hands. Let them flow from your heart through your arms, down through your hands and into the ball of light. You can begin to see or hear them in this orb; you might see the orb filling up with grey or black dense energy. When you feel it is full and you have got everything off your chest, push the ball away from you. Use your arms to push it away and say, "I don't wish to hold these feelings any more, be gone." Taking control is empowering.

Closing the chakras

Just as it is important to open your chakras to enhance the experience of receiving crystalline energy, so it is to close your chakras.

I do love actions that are teamed with intentions, so more often than not I trace a cross over each chakra in turn and say, "I wish to close this chakra." You can use the same method to close just one or two chakras if you like. For example, if you are a sensitive person, it may be a good idea to close your third eye and solar plexus chakras in big crowds of people, or in any uncomfortable situation. I often recommend to help little ones go to sleep.

At first, for a split second I worried whether or not I should be advising people to re-open the chakras that they had closed, that I was altering the balance, but the truth is the flow of energy through the body re-adjusts itself and we naturally open and close our chakras all the time. It's a case of being true to your intuition.

PULLING THE BLIND UP

You can open specific chakras by focusing on them. You may want to use the following exercise if, for example, you are nervous about a work presentation.

✳ Bring awareness to your throat, visualizing a ball of blue light there. You see a blind pulled down over it, so the blue light is not as bright as it could be.

✳ Slowly pull up this blind 100 percent so the light shines out unencumbered. You could add strength to your intention by following it up with an affirmation:

"I will speak clearly, from the heart, I am confident in my voice."

You could keep a little chrysocolla tumble stone, blue calcite, blue apatite or amazonite in your pocket to give you added support and confidence.

Balancing energy

There are many different crystals you can use to balance your energy. Clear quartz, amazonite, turquoise and agate are among my favourites.

A powerful visualization you can try is of purifying white light running through you while you hold the intention to re-balance your energy. This can also be a great tool for improving access to your intuition. By being grounded and balanced you are in the best spiritual state to receive.

REMEMBER

* Be open to your intuition and what it can bring you.

* Intention is everything.

* Trust in what you feel.

* Listen to your intuition. The first answer you feel is always the right one; it's your gut reaction.

CREATING A LIGHT LOOP WITH QUARTZ

This light visualization is to set intentions to release and re-balance.

In fact, it can be done with any pointed crystal or tumble stone. If you don't have clear or cloudy quartz, you could use a smoky quartz point or a rose quartz wand, and any tumble stone that you feel drawn to using. I have chosen to use quartz because it is a master healer and I want to represent the masculine and feminine energies. What's most important with this is the stated intention, "I wish to balance my energy systems", and the visualization of the cleansing white light.

Gather the things you will need:
– A clear quartz point, which has strong, purifying, masculine energy. The point directs pure light with laser-like precision. It is uplifting, amplifying white light that will cleanse and rejuvenate your energy, especially your masculine right side.
– A piece of snow quartz for its divine feminine energy. Gentle and nurturing in frequency, snow quartz looks after the crown and heart, and your feminine left side.

✳ Hold the crystals to your heart and open your heart. Surround the crystals with a bubble of white light and ask them to re-balance your energies. Then place the clear quartz point in your left hand, pointing toward you, and the goddess snow quartz in your right hand.

✳ Take a few deep breaths, feeling into your core. Pull the breaths down to the bottom of your belly and then make the next breath deeper than the last. Focus on nothing but the sound and feel of your breath.

✳ Bring attention to your left hand, opening your hand chakras (page 65) to take in the crystalline energy. Feel the laser direct a beam of white light into your hand. It travels up your left arm to your shoulders, releasing blockages and re-balancing as it moves through you. It travels down and across your chest, filling it up with white expansive light, through your heart and out through your right arm where the energy is amplified when it touches the goddess quartz, mixing with snow quartz energy. It travels back up your right arm, retracing its path to your left, creating a re-balancing light circuit. Each time the light sweeps through you, back and forth, feel it lighting you up from the inside, washing this beautiful white light through your upper body from where it filters down to your feet, washing you in cleansing light.

BALANCING YOUR CHAKRA SYSTEM WITH A CRYSTAL POINT

Choose a crystal point that you feel connected to and that matches your personal energy. A clear quartz point is a good one.

✳ Lie or sit in a comfortable space and hold the crystal point to each chakra in turn, with the point facing away from you. Start at your crown.

✳ Trust that the crystal is doing its work to re-balance that energy centre.

✳ Visualize a stream of energy leaving your body. This could be as a grey smog, a dense energy cloud or black tar – however you want to feel or see a blockage or build-up of energy.

✳ Do this in turn through all the chakras. While the crystal is in position, start to feel your energy slowly re-balancing and aligning within and around you.

Sounds simple? It really is.

ALIGNING WITH SELENITE

Another great exercise is to place a piece of selenite at your crown. My personal preference is to use a raw wand of selenite, pointing down toward my head. Selenite is a pure beam of white cleansing light; it's known as a light sabre in my home. This exercise helps to focus pure light inward and align your energy centres.

✳ Once you are comfortably lying down and relaxed, with the point of the crystal facing your crown chakra, visualize and feel a beam of white light being channelled through the crystal. This light touches the top of your head and trickles into your crown chakra, filling it up with white cleansing light.

✳ Let it flow down to your third eye, and then your throat. As it moves down, it creates a column of white light, cleansing and pulling everything into alignment.

✳ It continues to move down to your heart, your solar plexus, your sacral and finally your root chakra. Feel all your chakras connected by this beam of white light; flex them. Feel connected to them as they are part of you. You can contract this column of light and feel it as you follow it up out of your crown. See this white light column extending up and out to the cosmos, connecting you.

"I am aligned
and balanced."

Breath work and crystals

Breath work is at the centre of mindfulness and becoming aware of your energy. It can ground and connect you, so if you don't practise it regularly, now is the time to start.

It's good to pick a crystal that grounds your energy, maybe something black, brown or red as these are typically colours of grounding crystals. The best thing to do is to look at your collection of crystals and ask, "Which of you would like to ground me today?" The one that draws your eyes instantly is the one to hold.

Grounding crystals are good to hold when starting any breath work because they will pull your energy down to your root and the earth beneath you so you don't fly away but stay centred and balanced. The crystal I really recommend for this work is hematite. It has magnetic qualities and when I hold it, it literally pulls me down with a powerful force. Hold it to the bottom of your stomach to pull your breath down as deep as it can possibly go.

BREATHING IN CRYSTALLINE ENERGY

The energy fields around a crystal vary, much like the energy around our body. Some can be very subtle, some can pack a punch: it all depends on the intensity of vibration from the crystal. I ask that you draw on *all* of your senses to feel, see and sense crystal energy.

This exercise can be done with any crystal. Pick the one you feel most drawn to and take time to ground yourself first (page 57).

✳ Hold your crystal in front of you in your right hand.

✳ Connect with your crystal by gazing at every angle of it. Turn it over in your hand and follow the lines and markings within it. Open your heart and ask for your crystal to work to your highest good. Allow yourself to feel its energy. Once you feel connected, you may become aware of its aura, energy buzzing around it, or your hands may tingle. If you can't see its aura, imagine that you can. Use all of your senses.

✳ Start taking deep breaths and with each inhale breathe in the crystal's energy, merging it with your breath as if they had always been one.

✳ Close your eyes and follow where this energy wants to go within you. It may want to go up to your head or it might work its way to your heart. Just be aware and let it move where it wants to. Please trust that it is working on the areas that need release.

✳ When you feel ready to stop, open your eyes and write down any insights that come to you. Thank the crystal for working with you. You may want to run it under cold water to refresh it and put it away to rest.

Crystal journaling

I have kept notes since I started using crystals and meditating and found them extremely useful in developing my intuition. By tracking as much as you sense when working with crystals, you connect to them further and more wisdom comes through. It's a good practice to get into when starting this journey. I still keep a journal in my bag to note down any words or thoughts that come through during the day and through dream work at night.

To get your journal started, choose a crystal to work with and sit comfortably with your journal in front of you. Then work through the following steps:

✳ Make sure you are grounded (page 57) and have opened your chakras, especially your hand chakras (page 65).

✳ Set a clear intention, such as:
"I am open to this crystal's beautiful energies and wisdom."

✳ Take a pen in your chosen hand and the chosen crystal in the other, holding it to your heart to surround it with your heart energy – you might want to see and feel this as pink or golden light. You are programming it by asking it "to work to your highest good".

✳ Now rest this hand, still holding the crystal, to your side.

✳ Become aware of the crystal's energy flow through your palm chakra and up your arm. You may want to visualize it as a coloured light, or you may just feel it.

During this exercise, ask yourself these questions and write down any answers that come to you:

* Where does the energy want to travel to?

* What area of your body is it travelling to?

* How do you perceive its energy? How does it feel?

* Does it have a voice? If it does, or did, what does it sound like? Can you compare the voice to anyone you know?

* How does it wish to help you?

* Do you see or feel its energy as a colour?

* Does it bring any emotions to the surface?

* If yes, how can it help you to face and release them?

* Where does it wish to be kept?

* Do you feel you want to place it on any particular part of your body?

* Does it have any more messages for you or those around you?

* If you could sum up this experience in three words, what would they be?

Once you have finished this exercise, thank the crystal for its work and de-program it by telling it you are wiping it clean.

Be sure to write down as much as you can and practise this exercise with the same crystal over and over again. The more you do it, the more information will come through as your connection grows stronger.

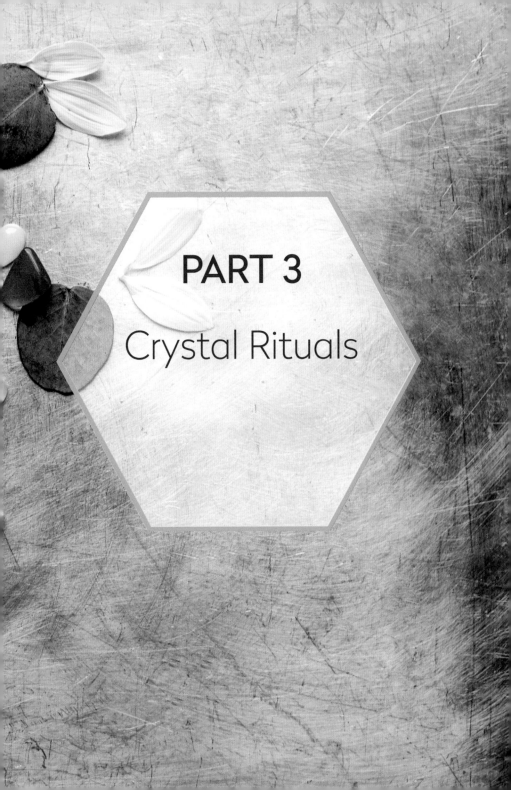

PART 3

Crystal Rituals

The power of crystal rituals

There are many wonderful ways in which you can use crystals
for healing rituals, from energizing your sacral chakra to
activating your confidence and power from within, calming a
frantic mind, helping you to expand into your heart energy and
experience love or to protect yourself and your space from
negative energy.

When you begin to work with crystals, you will sense how their
energy can help you at particular times, whether it's firing you up
to start a new project or grounding you when you feel a bit
disconnected. You can ask your crystals for help, both with letting
go of energy or emotions you no longer need and to call in
positive energy. In this section I have included some of my
favourite rituals, and I hope that you will feel inspired to explore
further as you get to know your crystals.

Energizing rituals

Over the next few pages you will be introduced to rituals that will help re-energize you. My favourite energizing crystals include carnelian, sun stone, citrine and fire agate or fire quartz.

ACTIVATE YOUR POWER

* Take some time to lie down in a space where you feel safe, with dimmed lights. Place one of the energizing crystals on your sacral chakra (page 21). You can also place a clear quartz on the ground above your head – so just above your crown chakra. Start to focus on your breath, making each inhale deeper than the last. Feel waves of blue light wash over you, relaxing every muscle, every cell. You feel yourself sinking into the bed/floor and being held and supported.

* Do this for a few minutes until you feel relaxed. Breathe in white light and breathe out any worries or anxieties. Feel your cells and chakras opening to accept the healing crystal energies.

* Focus on your crown chakra and visualize a beautiful white rose in bud there. Open the rosebud petal by petal and see pure white light bursting from the crystal at your crown, washing around your crown chakra, cleansing it of anything that does not belong there.

* Now bring your attention to your sacral chakra and see a spinning ball of orange light, which is your sacral centre. I want you to breathe in white light from your crown, and feel it running through your body. See it filling your sacral chakra, so that it gets brighter and expands outward. Become aware of the carnelian crystal sitting in your energy field and accept the crystal energy. Feel it coming from the crystal and into your sacral chakra, energizing it, sending a spark down there to ignite.

* Say this affirmation three times aloud:

"I reclaim and activate my power."

* Stay in the energy for as long as you wish, simply bringing your attention back into the room when you are ready to sit up gradually.

SUNSHINE VISUALIZATION

The sun is a powerful, masculine, energizing symbol, a life-giving source of energy. I do this visualization often, especially if I am outside in the sun, but it's not necessary to be outside. You can call the sun's energy to you.

✳ Feel the sun's rays dance around your body, feel the warmth and breath in them. Really focus on each golden breath and open every cell, every pore to this activating energy. Take the golden rays down through your crown.

Breathe and say, "Sun above my head."

✳ Feel the rays light you up from the inside, giving you what you need, and then pull those yellow rays through you and down into your heart.

Breathe and say, "Sun in my heart."

✳ See yourself lying in a sphere of golden sunlight, glowing inside out. It's so warm. You are re-setting your core, re-centring and re-energizing yourself with source energy. Sit with those feelings and that vision for as long as you need.

BOOSTING YOUR ENERGY FIELD WITH QUARTZ

You will need a clear quartz point for this exercise.

✳ Take the time to lie down in a safe space and draw your attention to the flow of energy in your body, moving in circular motions from your head down to your feet. Your crown lets in universal life-force energy and your feet take up earth energy. Become aware of this flow. If you can't feel it, imagine it.

Visualize and experience it moving in and around your body.

✳ Scan your body from top to bottom to identify an area where you feel energy is low or that needs a boost. Place your crystal there, the point facing toward your head. Leave it there until you feel the quartz raise your vibrations. Trust what you can feel and be guided by your energy.

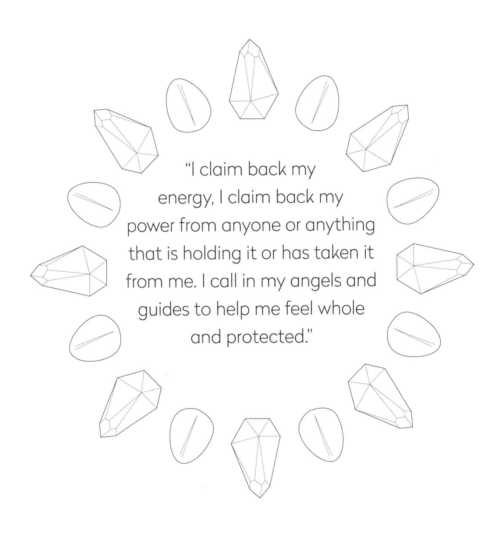

"I claim back my
energy, I claim back my
power from anyone or anything
that is holding it or has taken it
from me. I call in my angels and
guides to help me feel whole
and protected."

CLAIMING YOUR ENERGY

You can do this with the support of re-energizing and empowering crystals. Fire crystals stimulate the sacral and solar plexus chakras and these include carnelian, fire quartz, agate, red jasper, sun crystal and any volcanic crystals, such as tektite. Empowering crystals can be different for different people: some might find carnelian activating and empowering, while others find that rose quartz empowers their heart. Clear quartz is a good all-round crystal for empowerment.

✳ I would love you to relax, take a few deep breaths and centre yourself. Ground yourself by imagining roots growing from the soles of your feet deep into the earth.

✳ Imagine you are a magnet and you are going to summon all the energy you have given out through the day. You are attracting it back to you by saying (or thinking),

"I call my energy back to me from all places and people, through all energetic layers and directions of time, and so it is."

✳ Then I want you to see and feel all this energy zip back to you, like you are a huge magnet. Feel yourself absorbing it back into your energy field and recycling it.

✳ Say the following mantra three times:

"I claim back my energy, I claim back my power from anyone or anything that is holding it or has taken it from me. I call in my angels and guides to help me feel whole and protected."

Calming rituals

Visualizations, meditations and crystals can help to quiet the mind.

White, clear and blue crystals are considered calming, but you might find grounding crystals very calming for your energy and rose quartz soothing, and none of these are white, clear or blue.

My favourite calming crystals are amethyst, blue calcite, blue lace agate, lepidolite, howlite and sodalite.

I often give my five-year-old son a piece of sodalite when he is being overly emotional and finding it hard to say what is on his mind. It really helps by calming his mind, channelling his frustration out of his body and soothing his heart. You can team any of these crystals with clear quartz to amplify the intent. It literally doubles the dose of energy, supercharging it.

BREATHE AND SURRENDER

You will need a piece of amethyst for your crown; a piece of smoky or clear quartz to hold in your right hand; and your chosen calming crystal to hold in your left hand.

✳ Take the crystals to your heart, surround them with your light and ask that they help bring calm into your heart, and transmute any worries and anxiety into something positive.

✳ Take some time to lie down in a space where you feel safe, with dimmed lights. Place your amethyst just above your crown on the floor. Start to focus on your breath, making each breath in deeper than the last. Feel waves of blue light wash over you, relaxing every muscle, every cell. You feel yourself sinking into the bed/floor and being held and supported.

✳ Do this for a few minutes until you feel relaxed. Breathe in white light and breathe out any worries or anxieties. Feel your cells and chakras opening to accept the crystals' healing energies.

✳ Draw attention to your crown and see the amethyst light up, purple rays surrounding it, protecting your higher chakras, filtering down into your crown and washing purple light through your body.

✳ Stay with your breath; breathe deeply and slowly.

✳ Draw your attention to the smoky quartz in your right hand. Feel any negativity, anxiety, worry or trapped emotions run down from your body into your hand and through this crystal into the earth, which will transmute that energy into something good.

✳ Now turn your focus to the calming crystal in your left hand. Feel your palm chakra open and give that crystal's energy a colour. See that colour leave the crystal, enter your hand and travel up your arm. You can direct this energy to your heart to instil deep peace or you can let it be, letting it go where it needs to go.

Love rituals

Heart crystals are generally green or pink, but if a piece of celestite, moon crystal or selenite wants to work on your heart, go with it. There are so many loving crystals to choose from. My favourites are rose quartz, aventurine, jade, unakite, amazonite and rhodonite.

Self-love with rose quartz

How can we love ourselves more? This is one of the most important areas in our development and it is achievable with practice and a piece of rose quartz.

I am constantly re-affirming to myself that I am enough. General life and work struggles make me doubt myself daily, and comparisons on social media are not helpful.

The real truth is that we are doing enough, every day, by showing up and living this life. Of course, the day-to-day stuff can be difficult, not to mention all the heavy stuff we go through and mostly put ourselves through. But we are so hard on ourselves. Why?

We all strive to find love, to be loved and accepted, when really all we have to do is connect to our core, that bright shining light within, the divine. Then we feel love all around us. We just have to accept that love is already with us, but we choose to ignore it.

It's time to reach out to the cosmos and say, "Hey, remember me? I'm here and ready to connect deeper."

Open your heart and ask for the connection. Ask your guides to help you find it, to experience it. Then let them lead you in meditation.

MEDITATION JOURNEY TO VISIT THE ROSE GARDEN

Gather the things you will need:
– A candle to symbolize your light and crystals to help the connection.
– Rose quartz to place on your heart.
– Labradorite to open your third eye and bring protection and selenite at your crown to aid astral travel (page 148).
– A rose is not essential but is symbolic of the intention.

✳ Set the intention first by saying:

"I wish to take my energy to the rose garden on the spiritual planes. I ask that my guides support and protect me in this journey."

Mary Magdalene is a wonderful entity to call upon for loving support and guidance while you perform this meditation, but you can call upon any goddess you feel drawn to – Brigid, Aphrodite – or any of the angels.

✳ Light the candle and create or check in with your grounding cord (page 56). Lie down and hold your crystals to your heart, surround them in light and ask them to open up your connection to the divine and protect you. Then place them where you feel they need to be.

✳ Take as much time as you need to relax fully. See a beautiful white tunnel appear in front of you. This angelic portal will guide you to where you need to be; take a step into it. See your bare feet on the ground. Each step illuminates your path as you walk forward.

✳ Let yourself be led. Walk down the light tunnel and, in front of you, start to build up an image of the rose garden in your mind. See it appear like a painting being painted.

✳ What does it look like? What does it smell like? The colours are so vivid, unlike anything you have seen before. Ask your guides to meet you there and then feel their energy around you. Of course they are there ... you asked them to come.

✳ Give yourself a moment to stand inside the garden. Look around you at all the flowers in pinks, reds, peach colours. The air is alive, highly vibrational, you feel it buzzing. It gives you such comfort. Breathe that feeling in. Let the smell wash over you. The sun beams down on you, energizing you. Bring it down through your crown into your heart. Touch the rose quartz on your heart to check in with it. Tap it and ask to remember this feeling, embedding it in the crystal and your heart at the same time so you can keep that feeling and energy with you.

✳ Have fun with it. There is no right or wrong. Feel your guides around you and let them lead you somewhere. You might see or feel relatives and friends who have passed. Welcome them in, let them talk to you and hear them. What messages do they have for you? How do they think you could be loving yourself more? While you are reading this now, grab a pen and notebook, visualize it as you read and jot down any answers, symbols, feelings and words that come to you.

✳ When you feel ready to leave, give thanks and create a light tunnel in front of you. Step into it and follow a light at the end, which is your heart's light. Come back into your body and your core. Tap the rose quartz on your heart and check in with your body.

THE
ROSE GARDEN

This is a very special place to me. I am opening my heart in sharing it with you. It is where I first saw my dad in spirit through my dreams. He led me on a journey to a vivid garden full of the most wonderful roses, on spirit side, a place to respect and treat with reverence. I still go there often to talk to passed spirits, who tend to gather there. I think it's the perfect place for you to start your self-love journey with your guide, as roses, especially pink and red, symbolize love. So pure.

Recently, a beautiful light child I know, who astral travels a lot, spoke to her mother about a special rose garden on spirit side, saying that she saw me there in her sleep. Now I have never spoken about it to this darling child, so it goes to show it's there. Even though you may not be consciously aware of it right now, many of you will know this place and have visited it already. These words will bring the rose garden closer to you; they will resonate.

SELF-LOVE PRACTICE

✳ Hold some rose quartz and take a moment to relax your mind. Breathe in white light and breathe out any worries, doubts or anxieties, making each breath even deeper than the last. When you feel calm and centred I want you to do two things.

✳ First, surround yourself with a bubble of pink light – I call this the "love bubble" – and give yourself the love you need. It needs to come straight from your heart. Feel every cell, every pore, every muscle opening up in this pink light; breathe it in, soak it up. Sit or lie in this bubble for as long as you need.

✳ Then hold your arms up to the sky, palms facing upward (this is a receiving position), and say with love, intention and conviction:

"I am enough, I am loved, I am held, I surrender and release any fears that I hold, that are standing in the way of me achieving my soul's potential."

Afterward, light a candle for yourself and do something that makes your heart sing to mark this release – practise yoga, meditate, dance around your room, take a bath with salt and crystals, go for a walk alone in the woods, buy yourself a bunch of flowers. Do it for you; this is something to make your soul feel loved.

I always like to express myself creatively so I write, journal or more recently I have started to create beautiful floral crystal grids for myself (see page 112 for more explanation and examples).

Why don't you try one? Buy or pick some flowers (with permission) and collect natural items you love, such as twigs and pebbles, to use with your chosen crystals. I always lay out the crystals first, with one in the centre and other surrounding and branching off from it in maybe five or six branches, holding my intention while I position the crystals. Then I add my flowers and twigs and, taking a clear quartz wand (it's important that it's clear quartz), bind the grid (page 120). Don't worry about laying out a grid wrongly – there is no wrong. Just go with your intuition.

I then meditate on it and just absorb its loving, supportive energy. When I take it down, I bathe in the flowers while focusing on the intentions I set. The whole process is very beautiful and soothing.

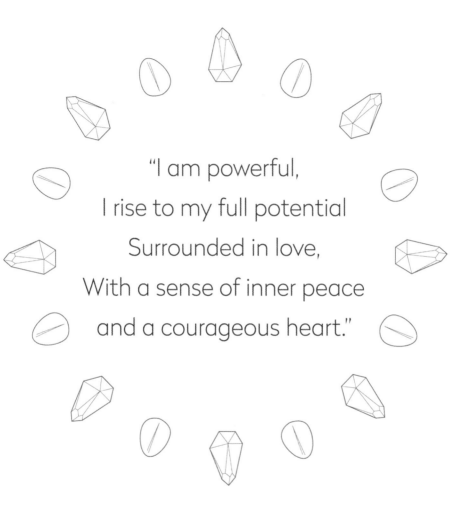

"I am powerful,
I rise to my full potential
Surrounded in love,
With a sense of inner peace
and a courageous heart."

Crystals and womb work

Despite it being a strong and miraculous organ, we all have a great deal of energetic trauma held in our womb. I want to share some important meditations and exercises that will help heal the "mother line" within us. This is our connection to every female within our family, and past families, through our ancestry line. We are all connected because we were all in our mother's womb down through the generations, and the same goes for each past life we have had as a woman. As you can imagine, the line is long.

Many nurturing feminine crystals are suitable for this purpose. Moon crystal and selenite, for example, are beautiful companions, motherly and supportive with the right gentle energy to guide and hold you. Jade and rose quartz have a soft energy that will help link your womb to your heart. Simply holding those crystals to your womb and setting the intention to cleanse and release that area will help. When you send intentional healing to this part of your body, you are not healing just yourself, but your family, too. Consciously or subconsciously, they will feel the effects. After sessions, women have told me that they felt discomfort and a release in their womb or sacral chakra and on that day their mother complained of random discomfort in the same area.

There are three very important factors to consider when beginning loving womb work:

1. How to connect your heart to your womb.

2. How to send love to your womb.

3. How to ignite and activate your womb.

I like to use carnelian and rose quartz for this work. Carnelian brings essential warmth to your womb. It is an energizing crystal and gives you courage, confidence, vitality and life-force energy. Rose quartz provides a gentler energy. You can use it in any form – tumbled, raw or carved. My choice is a carved rose-quartz egg, symbolizing new life, and a prompt to send love to your womb when you see the crystal on your bedside table. It will hold womb-healing affirmations and amplify them with love. It's gentle and nurturing and its soft energy will hold you on this journey. It will help you face any fears and blockages with a courageous heart, releasing things gently and in your own time.

Yoni eggs

The carved crystal egg is also known as
a Yoni egg, a tool to use internally to
send loving vibrations to your uterus.
I have been asked before for my
viewpoint on these, and I see nothing
wrong with them if you want to use
them in that way. But I do think that
energy is energy and you can feel that
energy by just placing the egg on top of
your womb, if your intention is strong
enough. It's like the idea of leaving
crystals on the window ledge for a full
moon to cleanse (page 39). They are still
going to feel the lunar energy, although
some would argue not with the same
force. But that's a personal opinion and
you should always go with your intuition

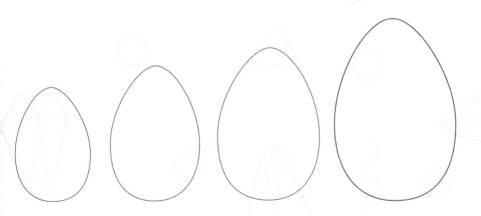

CONNECTING HEART TO WOMB

Begin this exercise by programming your crystals, rose quartz and carnelian.

✳ Hold the rose quartz to your heart and imagine your heart opening and surrounding the crystal in beautiful white light. Hold the intention in your head for your rose quartz to help you by healing your womb. Hold this intention for a few minutes.

✳ Hold your carnelian to your heart and ask it to work to your highest good, or you can be more specific by saying, "I ask that you warm and activate my womb."

If you keep your rose quartz in your bedroom, that's enough for its energy to work its magic, but you might want to place it on your heart or womb before sleep as you lie there. If you do, just call upon all your senses and go through the following steps to feel and see the pink crystalline rays seeping through your skin and travelling to the areas that need that loving light:

✳ Lie down in a quiet place where you feel safe and breathe.

✳ Place the rose quartz on your heart and carnelian on your womb.

✳ Focus on your heart. Feel it open, bright and beaming out pink light. You may want to see it as a pink flower, if that helps, opening petal by petal.

✳ Then I want you to build a bridge or cord of silver light from your heart, with the intention to connect your heart and womb. Watch it extend up and out, all the way down to your womb, connecting them both. Feel this bridge of silver light plug in to your sacral chakra and womb, illuminating them completely. Re-activating light travels down this cord to each chakra.

✳ When you are finished, remove the crystals and thank them for their help. You can do this exercise as much as you feel you need to.

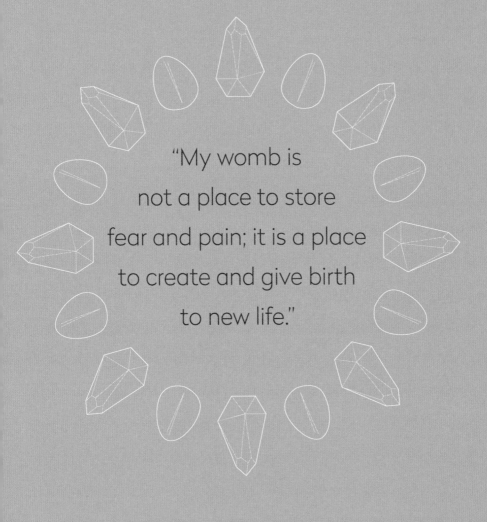

"My womb is
not a place to store
fear and pain; it is a place
to create and give birth
to new life."

Again, rose quartz and carnelian are the crystals of choice, but you can use any orange or red crystal instead of carnelian. First hold it to your heart and ask it to warm up your womb space.

✳ Take some time to lie down in a space where you feel safe, with dimmed lights. Place your rose quartz on your heart and your carnelian on your womb.

✳ Start to focus on your breath, making each breath deeper than the last. Feel each one working its way down to your womb to breathe fresh life into it. You may want to visualize it as pure white light, flowing in through your nostrils on every inhale and down into your womb, where it shines on anything that needs to be released. This could be held emotions that you had no idea were there.

✳ Feel every muscle and cell relaxing and releasing on each inhale. Feel yourself sinking into the bed or floor and know that you are held and supported.

✳ Do this for a few minutes until you feel totally relaxed. Continue to breathe in white light and breathe out any worries or anxieties. Feel your cells and body opening to accept the crystals' healing energy.

✳ Bring your attention to your womb. Imagine a closed pink rose there. I want you to open it petal by petal, with each breath as you breathe pink loving light into your womb space. Once this rose is fully open I want you to feel a glow of pink light there, radiating beautiful rays in front and behind you. Sit in this glow and feel the love.

✳ When you feel ready, become aware of the carnelian resting on your womb. Feel its weight as it rests on you. See and feel orange rays radiating from the crystal, and accept them, be open to them. Let them trickle down through your skin and muscle into your womb to fill it up. Watch the orange light wash through your uterus and down your fallopian tubes to wash around in your ovaries. Feel its warmth; feel it activating and warming every cell and tissue that it touches until your womb is a glowing ball of orange light. It is giving you exactly what you need at this time. Sit in this warm, activating orange light for as long as you feel you need to and say the following affirmation:

"I let go of any pain and trauma I am holding in my womb and replace it with love and forgiveness."

HEALING
NEEDED

It's important to note that everyone is different. This is not a quick fix. It is a way to connect with the energy in your womb and understand what is going on there. Once we become aware of our energy we are better equipped to balance and activate it. The more you work on this area, the more blockages will surface to be released.

Protection rituals

I don't like to talk of protection too much because talking about it brings the feeling of needing it and attracts the very thing we want to be protected from. We need to be conscious of our thoughts and live from our heart centre, not a place of fear. Worry and fear-based thoughts undermine our inner security. When we are grounded and at peace with ourselves, we are comfortable in our own skin and feel protected and safe. How do you view things? We have the ability to attract the very thing that we fear. Like attracts like.

We can have toxic emotions and ingrained belief patterns, obsessive thoughts that take time and practice to let go of. The more you work with energy and become connected, the brighter your light shines and you become more open. So it's important to know how to protect your energy from negative thoughts that may be projected at you, and from drainers.

You can be exposed to negative energy on a daily basis; just reading or watching the news is often an unavoidable culprit. Then there's such a thing as geopathic stress – the land your house sits on could be an area where the ley lines (energetic grids of the earth) are blocked, or the land could have past traumatic energy. You subtly feel and absorb all of these things. If you live in an area with a lot of power lines, or are around electromagnetic frequencies, that will have an effect. It all adds up.

The best ways to feel safe and protected are to ground yourself, be pure of heart and make sure you set good intentions.

Smudging is useful (page 34), wafting the smoke in all directions around your space and yourself, paying attention to the corners and furniture.

Crystals can do a lot, if not all, of the work but some useful visualizations strengthen the intent. There are many protective crystals with different vibrations – generally black in colour but, as you may know by now, this is not a rule. Some of my favourite ones are amethyst, a gentle, light, calming protector that absorbs negativity around you; labradorite, a great psychic protector that creates a shield around you, enhancing and keeping your senses open to feel but preventing anything from getting in; shungite, a purifying detoxifier that protects you from electromagnetic fields and all forms of negative vibrations; selenite, a beam of pure white light that illuminates your aura and holds you in light so nothing can touch you; celestite, bringer of angelic vibrations for a gentle but pure protection; black tourmaline, a good strong grounding and protective crystal.

"I trust that I
am protected.
I feel at peace and safe
within my body."

Energetic cords

Every day we attach unseen energetic cords to anyone with whom we have exchanges. These cords can build up and drain us over time. People who are particularly needy or volatile may drain you even more, some purposely but mostly without knowing. Those who are sensitive are more open to this and will feel it. You might hold in your mind now a person who you feel is doing this to you.

Sometimes in my workshops I ask participants to go into their hearts and imagine someone who is draining them. They are often surprised by who comes into their mind's eye. It could be a very close friend, husband, mother, father or the children. Participants are sometimes reluctant to cut cords but these cords are purely an energy exchange and cutting them does not sever the love you feel for these people. The exercise just establishes healthy boundaries. And you will find that although you cut cords, more will become attached. This is just the nature of energy. When we think of someone, we are connecting to them, so be aware of your thoughts, but also realize the importance of reclaiming your boundaries as often as you can.

CUTTING CORDS WITH SELENITE

A raw wand of selenite is inexpensive and a key crystal for your tool box.

✳ Hold it above your head. Imagine that it is a sabre of pure white light and sweep it down over yourself, from head to toe.

✳ As you do, set the intention that it is cutting any and all cords around you.

I feel cords deeply in my shoulder blades, and an acupressure spot under your left armpit has a tendency to hold hooks and cords. So make sure you swipe the selenite all the way around your body and under your arms.

CUTTING CORDS OF DRAINERS

If more than one person is draining you, repeat this exercise for each of them in turn.

✳ When you are calm and in a safe space, imagine the relevant person in front of you. See a golden cord of light connecting the two of you. It's good to notice where you see the cord; often it's in the heart but sometimes, if the person is a partner or ex, it's attached to the reproductive organs.

✳ Take a pair of golden scissors and start chopping that cord, starting at your end and snipping it into pieces, all the way to the person opposite you.

✳ Pick up the pieces and sweep them into an imaginary bonfire to the side of you. It could be a purple bonfire with violet flames – rays of this colour transmute negativity. Then watch it all burn away.

✳ You may find some resistance from the person opposite who may not want to let go, or he or she may re-attach afterward. If that is the case, send them your love and forgiveness and set strong boundaries. State very clearly that you give them their energy back. Draw a line between the two of you in the ground and say, "This is my space. That is your space. I do not wish you to re-attach or drain me any more." Say or think this with conviction. You can make the action with your hands, pushing the energy back to him or her, to strengthen the exchange. Then state or set the intention that you will not take any more of their energy.

RECLAIMING YOUR BOUNDARIES

Overbearing people can have a negative effect on you, but you can give them their energy back after an exchange.

Crystals that support healthy boundaries include shungite, black tourmaline and smoky quartz. If you have heavier, black crystals, it's nice to pair them with a softer, more feminine energy, such as snow or rose quartz, to balance them out.

✳ Visualize the relevant person standing in front of you and cut the connection cord as in the previous exercise. Then become aware of the two auras blending and merging into each other. Step away from this person and consciously take your aura out of his or hers. Give back the other person's aura saying,

"I give (insert full name) back his/her energy. I claim my aura for my own and retract it from (name) and so it is."

✳ Visualize the two of you as very separate entities with your auras detached and complete.

REMOVING TOXINS WITH CLEAR QUARTZ

I teach this technique often and it's wonderful to hear how much the visual helps people. They really see the black tar leaving their body. You can open your palm chakra and remove toxins without a crystal's help by pushing light through from your hand, but I find if you are working on yourself, this is the best way. You will need a clear or smoky quartz point.

✳ Place the cleansed quartz to your heart and say,

"I ask that you cleanse and remove any toxins and blockages in my body, replenishing me with pure white healing light."

✳ Place the quartz point at your left foot, pointing toward you.

✳ Set the intention to open your feet chakras to take in the crystal's energy.

✳ See a beam of bright white light come from the point of the crystal and enter your body. Let this light work its way up through your leg to your knee and thigh on your left side, pushing along stagnant energy as it goes. You may feel it as dense patches or see it as grey smoke or tar. The light is collecting the stagnant energy and pushing it up and around your body. It sweeps up to your chest, moves across your heart, lighting it up, and through your head, from where it starts to work its way down your right side, still doing its work. You feel the build-up. Keep moving down with it.

✳ When the light gets to your right leg and foot, open your right-foot chakras and feel and see a big purge of black tar. Let it run out of your foot and into the ground where it's transmuted.

✳ Take a step back and see this white light continuously pumping around your body, moving and cleansing. Let the psychic debris and tar go for as long as necessary to eliminate it all; there will be a lot. You might feel the flow getting lighter; you might see it slowly becoming clear. When clear light comes from your right foot, you will know it's done. Repeat this exercise as often as you can and over time you will notice a difference. The visuals will become stronger as you gain more of a connection to the energy flow in your body.

✳ Finish by setting the intention to close your feet chakras and seeing them shut. Then thank the earth for holding you and transmuting all of your toxins, toxic emotions, other people's negative energy and general psychic build-up.

Psychic shields

As well as carrying shielding crystals, such as labradorite, amber, aquamarine, black tourmaline, hematite, shungite, smoky quartz, citrine and apache's tears, you can do some simple visualizations.

✳ Bubble up – place a pure white bubble of light around you, making sure it seals under your feet, and fill it with dazzling white light. This protects you and creates a shield of pure light so that nothing negative can reach you.

✳ Surround yourself with mirrors – they have to encircle you and face outward.

Any negativity or lower vibrations that are aimed at you will bounce right back to the person who sent them. I often used to do this in meetings when I felt judgment would fall on me, and it worked a treat!

✳ Build a golden wall brick by brick to separate you from anyone who doesn't feel quite right energetically. I often do this when I am out and about in big cities, on public transport or standing in line. It's a good way to create a barrier.

TIPS FOR CREATING A SAFE HOME SPACE

✳ Position a clear quartz crystal on the ground in front of the entrance to your house, point facing away to absorb anything negative before it reaches your door.

✳ Place a piece of rose quartz on either side of your front door with the intention to protect your space. These two will let only loving vibes inside your home.

✳Choose four protective tumble stones, such as smoky quartz and/or black tourmaline. Place each crystal in the corner of the room you would like to

protect, stating that intention, and bind them with a clear quartz crystal or with a beautiful trail of light from your open-hand chakras.

✳ Visualize a golden cloche of light placed over the whole outside of your house to keep it in a protective vacuum. Check on it regularly and replace it when you feel it needs it.

✳ Bury clear quartz crystals around the perimeter of your garden in all the corners to strengthen the protective boundaries.

WASHING AWAY NEGATIVITY AT THE END OF THE DAY

I have got into the habit of making the front door to my house a screen for any negativity I have picked up during the day. As I walk through the door, I visualize walking through a curtain of purple light. It washes me of any psychic debris I have picked up from other people. I see and feel it wash off me into the ground. You can do this with any door. The key is the intention to wash yourself clean; the colour purple is symbolic of protection and the violet flame that transmutes energy.

Dragon energy

A house in London where I did a clearing exercise had very clogged-up ley lines, the land was saturated with heavy energy and the garden backed on to a graveyard. Needless to say, plenty of spirit visitors were about and it needed a lot of work to lift the vibrations. The usual sage, sound and crystal combination (page 34) was not enough. I gridded the boundary wall on the side that faced the graveyard with smoky quartz and black tourmaline that I dug into holes in the garden, and then continued to grid the rest of the garden. The central crystal – I felt in this case it needed one – was a clear apophyllite point, very cleansing and detoxifying. After doing all the necessary preparation and binding the crystals with light, I called in a mighty fire dragon to burn up the negativity in the ley lines; and an air dragon to blow away stagnant energy and replace it with fresh higher vibrations.

Dragon energy, much like unicorn and faerie energy, is a higher vibration than ours. Dragons are great earth healers and that is mostly how their energy is used and harnessed currently. So if you have a feeling that the land your home is standing on has stagnant energy, call in a dragon and ask for its help to cleanse your land. Welcome it in. Dragons love to be praised and appreciated.

The beautiful part of this house-clearing story concerns a three-year-old boy who lived there. For weeks he had been too scared to go to the far corner of the garden, which is where the patch of heaviest energy was to be found. The next day he ran over to it on his own and played happily, coming back to tell his mummy about a dragon he saw there.

PART 4

Crystal Grids

Working with crystal grids

A crystal grid is a group of crystals placed in a symmetrical pattern to direct focused energy toward an intention. The grid is created to support an intention and an affirmation can be added to affirm the result. For example, if you would like to create a grid to manifest a new job, you would use whatever crystals called to you – abundance crystals, such as citrine and pyrite, and luck crystals, such as green aventurine and jade, would be good – and then you would write the affirmation as though the intention had been fulfilled: "I was so happy when I got my new job."

There are no rules about which crystals to use. Mix as many as you like, although it's good to reflect your intention, as with the above example. If you are creating a heart-activating grid, you might like to select heart crystals such as rose quartz, rhodonite, pink kunzite and pink mangano calcite. A few examples of heart-activating grids are included in this chapter. A grid can be more powerful than asking one crystal to work to your highest good, since it involves a group of crystals working together on the same goal. Each crystal may have different properties that weave together what you wish to manifest.

Plenty of information is available online on how to go about creating grids, and there are many intuitive ways in which you can create something beautiful. Some people like to use grids based on sacred geometry, for example: the seed of life, Metatron's cube, flower of life, spiral, star of David, pentagon, circle and triangle. The geometry intensifies and moves the energy flow, which with the crystals makes for a powerful combination.

I let my intuition lead me. There is great beauty in creating something with pure, perfect spontaneity. The only guidelines I stick to are to have focus, way and desire crystals, as detailed throughout the following pages.

A focus crystal

This is a central crystal that the others are gridded around. It collects universal life-force energy and channels it through the grid, drawing it down and inward. Certain structures are usually preferred – a sphere, tumble or raw stone, a carved prism or point – but I trust the crystals to work together just as they should.

I tend to use prisms or a crystal with a point to direct the energy into one point. I also like to use spheres, as they send energy in all directions and so radiate the intention all around the room.

Way crystals

These are the smaller crystals positioned around the focus crystal to direct the energy flow. They shape the energy and amplify it. I like to use some crystal points to direct the flow toward or away from the centre, but you can use coloured tumble stones, too, or a mix. I start with an even number, six, positioned around the centre crystal, but you can go up to eight, ten or whatever you feel is necessary. It also depends on what kind of an impact you would like to make. What's important to remember is to focus on the intention that you have set each time you place a crystal.

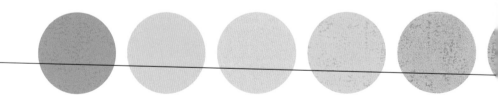

CRYSTAL GRIDS

COLOUR GUIDE FOR WAY CRYSTALS

✳ RED: for high energy and action, passion, the help you may need for getting on with important projects.

✳ PINK: for loving heart support whether for you or someone else, gentle focus, courage, nurturing support.

✳ YELLOW: for happiness, emotional release, joy, enhancing heartfelt communication.

✳ ORANGE: for action, persuasiveness, work on friendships.

✳ GOLDEN: for connection to the divine and guidance, help with commitment to projects and abundance.

✳ GREEN: for finding perspective, understanding, clarity.

✳ BLUE: for calming, help with communication, patience, reconciling differences, seeking forgiveness, honour.

✳ PURPLE: for help with creative intentions, manifesting magic and your dreams.

✳ WHITE: for attracting the power of the moon and the divine feminine, goddess energy and regeneration.

✳ CLEAR: for clarity, focus, intent, purity. Clear crystals can cleanse the grid ready for the new energies to be manifested and also amplify them.

✳ BLACK: for protection and mental focus, to help you stay alert.

✳ BROWN: for grounding the energies and intention.

Desire crystals

These are the crystals in the outermost position. They bring the power, the end goal, the manifesting of the intent and dispersing of energy to us. Take time to go inside yourself and really feel it when selecting these crystals, but please remember there is no right or wrong. Do not pressure yourself into worrying about what properties the crystals have. The right crystals will find you; as you know by now, they have a way of doing that. I think all crystals are desire crystals in a way; the whole grid is to support your intended desire.

The outer circle

There may be a need to protect this gorgeous grid you have created from outside influences and you can do this by forming a circle around it. I have done this before with flower petals or salt, but you can use a protective visualization if you prefer. Hold your hands around the grid, one on either side, and open your hand chakras with intention. Imagine golden light flowing out of your hands and surrounding the grid like a cloche, filling it with love and golden light to protect the intentions you have set.

Programming your grid

Once you have selected and cleansed your crystals, hold them to your heart to program them, stating your intention, either out loud or in your head:

"I program my grid to ..."

Focus on your intended outcome. Visualize it and hold the emotion of it in your mind.

Binding the grid

When you have created your grid, you need to connect the dots and join the lines. Take a clear quartz point in your hand. Start at the focus crystal and work outward, moving the point over the crystals to connect them like the spokes on a bicycle wheel and in triangle shapes, going back over yourself to make sure every single crystal is connected to the centre. Once I have gone all the way around I always finish in the centre with a rather theatrical flourish of my wrist, directing the light upward. All the while you are doing this, hold the intention for the grid in your mind.

Instead of the clear quartz point, you could use a twig, a stick with a crystal bound on the end, a crystal wand or another crystal point. Choose based on emotion. You could also open your palm chakras and visualize white light coming from your hands and use that to bind and direct the flow of energy.

Personal touches

Colour, affirmations and images can add strength to a grid. Here are some ideas for adding a personal touch.

* PHOTOGRAPHS
Place a relevant photograph underneath the focus crystal. This could be of a person to whom you want to send some healing or a destination you would like to visit or support. You can send healing to places, too. If you wish to manifest a happy family life, you could find one of those classic catalogue images of a family sitting around laughing with each other. If you would like to manifest some money, you could place some money under the crystal with an affirmation.

* NATURAL ELEMENTS
I like to combine these in as many ways as I can. You can use anything you find in nature – pine cones, twigs, berries, leaves. Shells and sand are a lovely nod to the sea and the healing power of water. Flowers and fruit add a beautiful energy and colour; feathers add the air element.

* AFFIRMATIONS
To write an affirmation on a piece of paper and place it under the focus crystal will really help with the end result. Write your affirmation as if it has happened. For example, if it's a heart-healing grid, you could write:

"My heart feels so full and happy."

If it's a calming grid to help you sleep, you could write something like:

"My heart, mind and body are relaxed."

Sacred ceremony

The way I approach creating crystal grids is with great ceremony because, in essence, the process is as important as the grid – being mindful and taking time to sit with the crystals, flowers and gathered offerings from nature; thanking each element for being a part of the ceremony, connecting with it; picking each flower with love and placing each one thoughtfully within the grid; using all senses; having a big, grateful, open heart and deep respect for the ceremony.

These grids take centre place in my workshops and sessions. Not only are they a beautiful focal point, they draw you in and welcome you.

They activate your energy in new ways, which at the time you might not realize fully, as they are full of wishes and intentions for healing. It is a wonderful thing to meditate on them.

Nature's spirits and the elementals are happy to be offerings if it means that we take a moment to marvel at their beauty and healing messages, if we give them the time, if we really gaze at them and listen to each flower's story of Mother Nature's love.

First, I gather my intentions of what I would like to create, perhaps a safe space for women to come and gather around. It could be a heart-expanding grid focused on release, or a grounding and earthing celebration.

I then call in the elements, asking for wind from the north, fire from the east, water from the south and earth from the west. I make sure I honour each element by representing it. For air, I call it in, invoking the element of wind that is all around us. You may wish to add feathers as a visual symbol of air. For earth, I dedicate the crystals and flowers. I have a small bowl of water close by the circle, and candles represent the fire element. You can also call in deities, angels and goddesses, whoever's energy you feel you need to be present to support you and the ceremony. I smudge with palo santo or sage (page 34) to cleanse the area, the crystals and grid space, and if I feel called to it, I sing or chant. Then I program the cleansed crystals.

A lot of the time I create these grids to honour myself and my soul and the journey I am on. It is important to stop and breathe into how far you have come and recognize all that you have achieved, because it is vast. We scale mountains within us every day; we ride the waves of energy flowing through us, in constant motion. We do so much every day, our bodies do so much every day that we owe ourselves some quiet time to sit with our spirit and give thanks for the support.

Take a moment right now to feel into your heart and ask yourself, "How can I honour myself more?"

A CRYSTAL GRID TO HONOUR YOURSELF AND YOUR SOUL

Gather the things you will need:
– Your favourite flowers as a treat; go out in nature to gather leaves, twigs, berries; collect beautiful, natural things that you love. You will need a good mix of items to express yourself creatively.
– A small collection of crystals that ask to be used in this ceremony – a focus crystal and as many way crystals as you feel you need (page 116). You could reach for your favourite crystals at this time or pick out the ones that most represent you energetically.
– A clear quartz crystal point to bind the grid.
– Some candles.
– Your journal or a notebook and pen.

✳ Hold the selected, cleansed crystals to your heart or third eye, take three deep breaths and say,

"I program this crystal grid to honour my soul, my heart and my journey."

Set an affirmation if you wish, example below. Write it down and put it next to the grid.

"I celebrate all the beautiful ways that I am me. I am forever proud of the ways that I step up and am present during this earthly experience. And I thank my guides past, present and future for their love and support through this journey."

✳ Start the grid by setting down the focus crystal with intention. Feel it in your heart and know that what you are creating is just for you – no right or wrong.

✳ Next lay the way crystals around the focus crystal. You could lay them on top of your flowers and leaves or put the flowers and leaves in between the crystals. Be as big and as bold as you like – whatever makes you happy. Make sure you place the crystals with your intention in mind, and bind the grid with light, from your quartz crystal point or your hands.

✳ Once you have set everything up, add some candles and sit with it, breathing in its light and love, focusing on the intention to honour yourself in that moment and every moment. Feel this grid taking on an energetic life of its own. You have given it life. Connect and gaze at each element and imagine an energy field around it, around each crystal, each flower, and on every inhale take that energy and love up through your nose and breathe it deep into the seat of your soul. Breathe it into your heart and down to your core. Sit with that sensation and see what feelings arise. You might smile at the deep gratitude you feel. Other feelings may surface and if they do, just acknowledge them; ask yourself how you can serve your soul better. Take your notebook and jot down any thoughts or feelings that come to you.

CRYSTAL GRID FOR
CREATIVE ACTIVATION

Gather all the things listed for the grid to honour yourself (page 120). Select sunshine yellow and orange crystals, such as citrine, amber, carnelian, clear quartz, orange calcite, tiger's eye and pyrite; and yellow, white and orange flowers, petals and leaves.

If you like, dab some tangerine or lemon eucalyptus citrus oil on your pulse points and breathe it in while creating the grid. The oil is stimulating and will support the crystal work you are doing.

✳ Take a quiet moment to bring awareness to your sacral chakra, your creative centre just below your navel. Place your palms there to feel the connection. Connect with your breath and pull each breath down into the chakra. Visualize it as a spinning orange sphere if that helps. Breathe into this orange sphere, and as you connect with it feel how fast or how slowly this energy centre is moving. Once you have sat with these feelings for a little while, slowly open your eyes, grab a pen and paper and ask yourself these questions:

1. How can I express myself more creatively?

2. How am I holding myself back?

3. How can I be more open to the creative flow of energy?

✳ Hold the selected, cleansed crystals to your heart or third eye, take three deep breaths and say,

"I program this crystal grid to activate my sacral chakra and connect me to my creative flow."

Set an affirmation if you wish, example below. Write it down and put it next to the grid.

"I am open to the universal creative flow; I am able to express myself creatively in all the ways that I need to."

✳ Then you can start constructing your grid in the same way as described for the grid to honour yourself (page 120). Be as creative as you can be. You have come from a place of introspection and have opened yourself up to the flow of creativity. When you are sitting with your grid, breathing in its energy and love, remember to focus on your intent and your sacral chakra.

CRYSTAL GRID FOR THIRD EYE AND HIGHER GUIDANCE

Gather all the things listed for the grid to honour yourself (page 120). Select purple and indigo crystals to connect with your third eye, such as labradorite, amethyst, clear quartz, fluorite, lapis lazuli, moon crystal, sodalite, apatite, Herkimer diamond, selenite; and purple and white flowers, petals and leaves. If you like, add white feathers, mirror tiles and anything else you can find that inspires you.

You could dab some clary sage oil on your pulse points to breathe in and bring calm feelings while you are creating the grid. It may help to open your third eye to higher guidance.

✻ Take a quiet moment to bring awareness to your third-eye chakra, your psychic intuitive centre just between your eyebrows.

✻ See a spinning indigo sphere there and open it fully. See its light beaming out in front and behind you. Then see a beam of cosmic white light resting on your crown and imagine a flower opening on the top of your head to let this light stream in, bringing down new fresh white light, activating your crown

and expanding it. Pull that stream of light down to your third eye to cleanse and activate the chakra.

✻ Hold the selected, cleansed crystals to your heart or third eye, take three deep breaths and say,

"I programme this crystal grid to connect me consciously to my higher self and bring a deep connection to myself and my guides."

Set an affirmation if you wish, example below. Write it down and put it next to the grid.

"My third eye is open, I connect with and welcome my gifts, intuition and any higher guidance that wishes to be known."

✻ Then you can start constructing your grid in the same way as described for the grid to honour yourself (page 120). Be as creative as you can be. You have come from a place of introspection and have opened yourself up to the flow of the universe. When you are sitting with your grid, breathe its energy and love into your third eye.

CALMING GRID FOR THE HOME

This is a lovely way to bring soothing energy into your home or into your bedroom to aid restful sleep. While we sleep we are more sensitive to crystal energy, so be wary of how many and which crystals you have at your bedside. People have told me that they are having such active dreams they can't sleep well, and when I've asked what crystal they have on their bedside table, I've known before they answered that it was selenite. This crystal opens your crown and aids astral travel – not conducive to a good night's sleep. Any high-vibrational crystals should not be in the bedroom and especially not under your pillow, unless you like it, of course.

So if this grid is for the bedroom, choose your crystals carefully. Don't mix too many and keep a good balance. A rose quartz focus crystal would be perfect. You could dab some relaxing lavender oil or frankincense on your pulse points and breathe it in while creating the grid.

Gather the things you will need:
– A round or tumbled focus stone for a gentle, radiating energy.
– Pink loving crystals, such as rose quartz and mangano calcite.
– Calming crystals such as lepidolite, blue lace agate, blue calcite and howlite.
– Grounding crystals in brown or red, such as black tourmaline, hematite or red jasper.
– Dried lavender.
– A clear crystal quartz point to bind the grid.

✳ Hold the selected, cleansed crystals to your heart or third eye, take three deep breaths and say,

"I program this crystal grid to bring calm, soothing energy into my home."

✳ Place the focus crystal and then lay the way crystals around it (page 120). Scatter the lavender in between. Make sure you place the crystals with intention, and then bind the grid with light, whether from your quartz crystal point or your hands. Set an affirmation if you wish, example below. Write it down and put it next to the grid.

"I am calm and centred within my space and my space reflects that."

✳ Once you have set up the grid, leave the energies to settle and flow through the room, giving off the calming effect you wished for.

PROTECTION GRID

You could dab an earthy grounding oil, such as sandalwood, cedarwood or patchouli, on your pulse points and breathe it in while creating this grid. The more grounded you are, the safer and more protected you feel within your body and in your space.

Gather the things you will need:
– Protective and grounding crystals – anything black, brown or red, such as black tourmaline, hematite, red jasper, red tiger's eye, shungite, labradorite.
– Twigs, bark, pine cones or similar items from nature to bring in the earth grounding element.
– A clear crystal quartz point to bind the grid.

✳ Hold the selected, cleansed crystals to your heart or third eye, take three deep breaths and say,

"I program this crystal grid to protect my space, my home and all who live here from all forms of harm."

Set an affirmation if you wish, example opposite. Write it down and put it next to the grid.

✳ Place the focus crystal, keeping your intention in mind, and then lay the way crystals around it. Scatter the items from nature in between, or you could place the crystals on top of them. Then bind the grid with light, with your quartz crystal point or your hands.

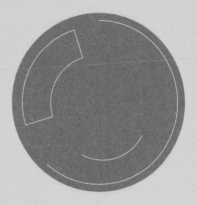

"I trust that
this space is
protected. I feel safe and
at peace within my
home."

A CRYSTAL GRID TO WELCOME NEW LIFE

This can be used in a range of ways – to welcome new ideas, a new burst of creativity, a new job, a baby – and it is very cleansing of your sacral chakra if you set the clear intention to cleanse as well as to love and honour it.

Gather the things you will need:
– A crystal egg to symbolize the womb and new life.
– A full rose to symbolize you and your heart centre.
– Flower petals. Make sure you thank the flowers for being part of your ceremony as you pick their petals.
– A small handful of natural Himalayan rock salt.
– Tumble stones, clear quartz, rose quartz, carnelian, selenite. You choose which ones you want, but it would be good to have an even number for the grid.

✳ Start by placing the crystal egg and rose in the centre and build the crystal grid up around them. Lay a small inner circle, which is representative of your womb, with flower petals, and as you do so hold your heart open and set the intention to welcome fresh energies into your womb and to release old energy or belief patterns you have held there that do not serve you. Say this womb-healing mantra:

"I am connected to the creative flow of life, it flows up through my feet, connecting my chakras, aligning them to my spiritual and creative potential to be all that I am, all that I am capable of and all that I came here to do."

✳ Next make a circle of rock salt around the inner circle to act as a barrier, cleanser and protector.

✳ Around the outside, add your crystals in any grid pattern you like. If you have any crystal points, focus them into the centre. Place each crystal with the intention to heal your womb space.

✳ Say the affirmation on the opposite page seven times – the divine number of completion – all the time focusing on the intention to heal yourself and to re-connect.

"I welcome new life,
I welcome new ideas,
I welcome love."

Meditation in a circle of crystals

In effect, by meditating within a grid of crystals, you are gridding yourself – you become the focus crystal, the central point. I love doing this as often as I can because the feeling of channelling and building up the crystalline energy through my body is amazing. The more you do it, the more intense it feels.

You can vary the crystals for a different feeling. For example, if you use rose quartz, the energy is very gentle; if you use high-vibrational crystals, such as aura quartz or spirit quartz (see image on page 152), the energy is heightened and more intense. You can add clear quartz or calcite to amplify and boost the effect. Choose raw, tumbled or crystal points, but if you use points, please face the point toward you because this directs the energy to you. In truth, there are no set rules and you may use whichever crystals you are drawn to, so long as your intention and the process by which you pull up the energy through your body is clear.

The first time I ever did this meditation I used my intuition, selecting eight crystals. I felt it was important that they were either all the same or in pairs so they could be placed opposite each other to enable their energy to communicate and balance out. I chose two clear quartz points, two pieces of celestite and four large spirit quartz points – all high-vibrational because I needed that energetic lift. Celestite has angelic frequencies and the clear quartz amplified the overall effect. I'll walk you through this exercise (page 134) with rose quartz because you can buy it inexpensively in raw form or as tumble stones.

HEALING CRYSTAL CIRCLE MEDITATION

This calls for a lot of focus and you may have to try it a few times before you really feel the intensity of the energy flowing into your root and up through you.

You need four pieces of rose quartz and four clear quartz points, or you can use eight pieces of rose quartz if this feels right.

✳ Set a circle of rose quartz big enough for you to sit in. Do this mindfully, placing each crystal with the intention to give you what you need.

✳ When you feel calm and centred, sit in the crystal circle. Make a connection with each crystal by looking at it, talking to it, asking for its help.

✳ When you feel ready, close your eyes and take a few deep belly breaths. In your mind's eye connect to the crystals around you. Welcome their energy into your root chakra. On each breath in, feel the energy flowing from each crystal into your root chakra. Feel it gathering there and keep breathing it in to fill you up. Take a moment to strengthen the connection in your mind to each crystal and see its energy field, its life-force energy flowing from it into you.

✳ Once you feel your root is full, gather that crystalline energy, take it up to your sacral chakra and slowly move it up to your solar plexus. Each time you move it up, see and feel the crystals around you pushing more of their energy into your root chakra.

✳ Keep moving this energy up through your chakras – your heart, your throat, your third eye. It lights them up with love. You may see a colour as this energy takes form.

✳ When at last you bring this energy up to your crown, you might sense an intense pressure there, a feeling that it needs to leave your body and could explode out at any time. Hold it as still as you can.

✳ Slowly open your crown chakra by seeing a closed white flower there on top of your head and opening it petal by petal. When it's fully open, feel an intense release of energy as it pools in golden light and blasts out of your crown. You can take this golden crystalline light down and let it shower you with healing. Be open to its rays, really feel the warmth and activation as it seeps through your skin. Alternatively, if someone you know needs healing, see that person in front of you and shower him or her with this golden energy. See the person smiling, cells opening to accept it. You could also send the healing to a place that's in need of it, by seeing the place in front of you and showering it with the golden light.

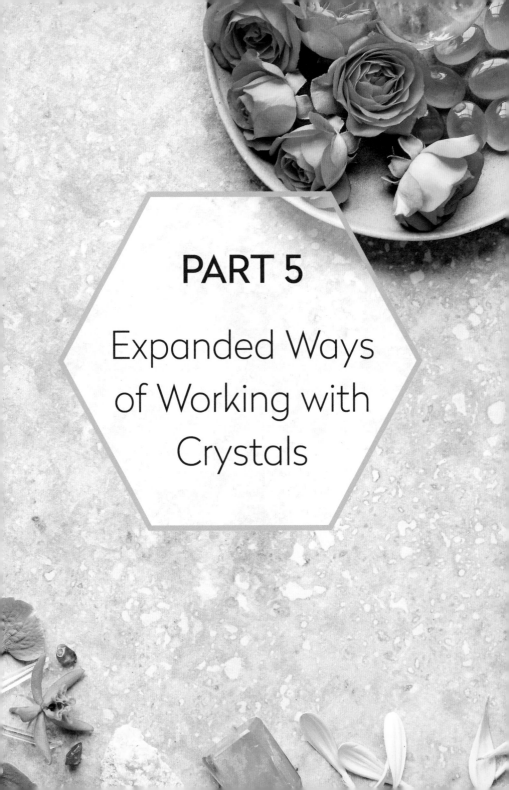

PART 5

Expanded Ways of Working with Crystals

Expanded ways of working with crystals

The ways we work with crystalline energy are rapidly changing and evolving as we raise our vibrations and collective consciousness. Crystals can do so much more than we realize and we can call on their powers without even being in their physical presence or owning one. If you want to feel the energy and protection of a certain crystal, you can call it to you; or you can connect through a photograph to feel its effects. This is what you do when you buy a crystal online.

I recently held a large piece of red quartz. It was clear quartz coated in iron, which gave it the red colour and made it extremely grounding. Upon holding it, I realized that its heavy, earthy energy was just too much for me. My whole hand went numb and that numbness crept up my arm until I felt I was being dragged down so deeply into the earth that I put the crystal down. At that time, it was just too much for my own gentle and airy energy.

Later that day I was telling someone about this red quartz and how it had made me feel and my hand started to go numb again. I was nowhere near the crystal at the time, but I had formed a connection with it and just by talking about it and thinking of it I was forming an energetic link to it and its effects. So calling a crystal to mind with the intention of connecting with it is all you need to do at times.

Putting your energy into a crystal

Crystals give us wonderful energy to use, but they can also hold our energy, recording thoughts, feelings and emotions. In essence, they are record keepers and like to hold intentions and affirmations. This is how crystals have been used through the past, as keepers of important universal and cosmic knowledge.

I have a lot of beautiful examples of this. One was when I was visiting a gorgeous soul in her last phase of life at a hospice. I was there to support her in her crossing and to connect her with her lost loved ones to aid the process. What followed was a beautiful and sacred exchange with her husband and sister, who had passed but were waiting to embrace her with love and lead her into the light. Moments like this are very emotional but remind us that love is eternal and so is the soul. She talked about her crystal collection, showing me a rose quartz heart. I asked that she place that quartz to her heart, and that she put a bubble of pink light around it, filling it with her love. She put her energy and vibrations into it, just through intention and visualization. I really felt that this crystal was for her daughter. It was a parting gift, so that whenever the daughter needed to feel her mother's love around her, she could place that rose quartz heart to her own heart and feel her mother's warmth when she was gone in the physical sense.

The energizing I describe on the next page is something I do for my child, too. I recommend it to parents whose child may be clinging to them, and to those who have someone close who suffers from any kind of anxiety.

ENERGIZING A CRYSTAL

* Take a crystal you love. You may want to select a loving crystal – something carved into a heart is good – or a protective crystal, but it's up to you.

* Hold it to your heart, preferably in front of your child so they can understand what you are doing, and talk them through it, too.

* Imagine your heart opening and shining your light all around this crystal, holding it in a bubble of your light.

* Put all your loving thoughts and feelings into this bubble of light and watch and feel the crystal absorb it. You might want to imagine the crystal lighting up.

* Hold the intention that you are filling this up with your loving energy you have for your child.

* Breathe your love into that crystal. Whisper your loving words to it.

* Hold this for as long as you feel you want to: a couple of minutes is enough.

* Then thank the crystal and pass it to your child, letting her know that if she is ever scared or worried, she can reach for the crystal in her pocket and know that mummy or daddy is with her. The crystal holds mummy or daddy's special magical energy.

Sending your energy on

We have spoken about putting your energy into a crystal for someone to take comfort from you, but now I want to talk about sending your energy on.

I attended a retreat where a very graceful and powerful shaman spoke to my heart about what I am about to share with you. His name is Shaman Durek. He told us about our ability to send our energy on to a sacred site or calm space to download and activate the energy within us in order that we may feel the benefits of that place energetically. He then asked us to teach and share this practice. So, in the meditation below I have interpreted the shaman's practice in my own way, by adding my own magic to it, because it struck me as a wonderful meditation to do with crystals.

It is much like what people do when they have a safe space or a happy place to retreat to in their mind. For example, when I'm feeling stressed or need to replenish, I take myself away to the amethyst caves.

MEDITATION TO TAKE YOUR ENERGY TO AMETHYST CAVES

✳ Find your sacred space and sit and breathe into your core.

✳ Set the intention to take your energy to an amethyst cave.

✳ Visualize it, see it cascade over your head and surround you. Start to become aware of what the energy feels like, washing over your whole body.

✳ See the purple glow from the cave surround you and penetrate every cell and fibre of your being. You might feel tingly, safe, held and loved.

✳ Welcome that energy into your crown and wash it through your body.

✳ Tap your heart or third eye and ask to download and activate these feelings inside you.

You can visit this cave again and tap your heart or third eye to re-activate these calm feelings in your daily life whenever you need a crystalline boost.

MEDITATION TO TAKE YOUR ENERGY TO A LIVING ROSE QUARTZ TEMPLE

✳ Find your sacred space and sit and breathe into your core.

✳ Set the intention to take your energy to a rose quartz temple or cave.

✳ See a beautiful beaming white tunnel of light appear in front of you, and step inside it. Feel the white light holding and supporting you. In the distance see a pink light, which gets bigger as you walk toward it, so big that it engulfs you in pink rays. You are walking into your heart's cave.

✳ Visualize it and feel it through all your senses. This is your heart space. Start to become aware of what the energy feels like, washing over your whole body. What does it look like?

✳ See the pink glow from the cave surround you and penetrate every cell and fibre of your being.

✳ Welcome that energy into your body through your crown and wash it through your body.

✳ Tap your heart and ask to download and activate these feelings inside you, the feelings of love and peace, stillness and connection.

Crystal skulls

It took me a long time to understand crystal skulls and why they are here with us. I was never drawn to them – looking at them scared me because skulls are associated with violence and death. That began to change when I met a huge quartz crystal skull, who was such a force of nature that I now look at them with the reverence they deserve.

As soon as I saw this skull I was captivated. "He" impressed the need for me to place my third eye to his, and when I did, it was as if I was sucked into a vacuum. I was in space. It was dark and stars whirled around me. I saw earth below me and all the golden webs around the planet, the ley lines and grids. They were being re-knitted and healed. I saw my place in it all and gained great clarity and understanding. He pushed a tornado of swirling energy through my whole body, linking me to the earth and creating golden vortexes to heal, showing me mystical beings I had never seen before, such as beautiful golden unicorns. From that moment I was hooked.

Ancient people, including the Mayans, the Aztecs, Native Americans and other indigenous people around the world, passed down stories of the crystal skulls through millennia. They first surfaced in Atlantean and Lemurian times, periods in ancient history when people believed in islands and continents that are now lost. According to tradition, the priests and priestess of Lemuria programmed the crystal skulls with wisdom that they had channelled from source and other star beings.

During those times a lot of spiritual gifts were misused for personal gain, power and ego. The knowledge of the crystals was so great and powerful it needed to be protected from those who would use it in the wrong way. It is written that there were 13 master crystal skulls, all of which were buried to protect the wisdom. They were assigned guardians and many of them lie buried with their secrets still. The legend goes that at a pivotal time in human history these 13 crystal skulls will surface to mark a new era, coinciding with a great shift from the old paradigm into a new world.

Some people talk about the power of multiple skulls working together, 12 skulls circling a master skull, which links them and intensifies their energy. I have witnessed the power of crystal-skull grids, which unlock more of the skulls' collective potential for both activation and change.

If you feel pulled to work with crystal skulls, you may have a history of working with them in your previous lives. I have experienced a past-life journey where I saw myself as a Mayan warrior. I was led to an old overgrown temple in the jungle where, after journeying down many tunnels, I came to a sacred inner temple filled with light language and codes all over the wall. There I saw myself in spirit sitting with a huge skull, which looked like clear quartz but was of a different energetic resonation, a much higher vibration than I have felt before. I understood this to be an energy we are not ready for yet, but which will be coming back to earth soon. I felt strongly that I was a guardian of this skull. I saw myself burying it and my soul had stayed behind to watch over it.

In essence, crystal skulls are very wise teachers that connect us to cosmic knowledge, past, present and future. The potential they can unlock within us is incomparable. Crystal skulls are very personal to the individual. They have different personalities and often very specific areas that they want to work on with you. They come to people for a host of different reasons. I have known skulls want to help past-life experiences to surface gently. They have come to give inner remembrance and confidence. I have a range of crystal skulls and, no matter the size, I find them equally as powerful as each other.

How to work with crystal skulls

When meeting a crystal skull for the first time, it is important to interact with it in a way that feels right to you. The process is very similar to using any crystal. You have to connect with it, hold it to your heart and listen to it.

I have found they do like being placed with the base flat on your body. You may want to start by placing it on your third eye, or you may wish to gaze into its eyes to gain a deeper connection with it. Another good way to connect with a crystal skull is to place it above your crown, facing you as you lie down.

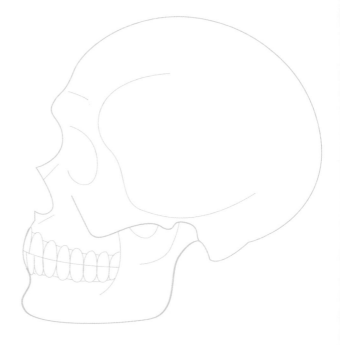

CHANNELLING A CRYSTAL SKULL

If you don't have a crystal skull, don't worry. You can gaze at the master skull at the centre of the grid, in the image on page 145.

✳ It is important to make contact and set your intentions clearly in a ceremony. This kind of energy and power deserves honour and respect. Light a candle and state your intentions aloud, talking to the universe:

"I wish to connect with the powers that be, elemental, universal and planetary energy. I speak to spirit and ask for that connection. Guide me to the place I need to be at this time. I respect and honour your infinite wisdom."

✳ As you are saying these words, gaze at the crystal skull in front of you, whether it is a physical skull or a photo of one. Imagine spirals of indigo light leaving the skull's eyes and entering your third eye, opening and expanding it. Let its energy wash over your body and hold you in a bubble of blue light. Ask it to activate and download any energy codes that you need.

✳ Feel yourself being pulled into the skull. Let your energy merge with it. You can visualize yourself inside it, looking around the inside. How does it feel? Let the energy give you what you need. You just need to hold yourself in an open, receptive state. Feel all of your cells opening like little bursts of light, ready to receive whatever messages that come.

✳ Afterward, be sure to make a note of all your feelings, any emotions, visions, sounds, smells or colours that came to you during this.

✳ Repeat this exercise as often as you feel necessary, each time surrendering to the bigger picture. Try to feel the universe, planets and all the stars move through you because they are inside you and you are them.

Crystals and astral travel

I'm going to let you in on a little secret. We all travel astrally and work in other realms and dimensions all the time; we are just not conscious of it. A lot of people can tune in through their sleep, either practising lucid dreaming or by recalling it when they wake. If you knew the small piece of us that is actually present in our body, you would be amazed. We are multi-dimensional beings, doing so many magical things.

I am consciously aware of the pieces of my soul travelling and I can follow the golden cords to where I am and what I am doing. It's called bi-locating. I do this during the day consciously. When I draw my attention to these parts of my soul, I can be aware of multiple realities. It takes a lot of focus in the beginning, but it's not impossible for you to do. The most I am aware of bi-locating is to four places at once and in each one I have been aware of what I am doing, what I am saying and to whom.

For example, my son and I often visit people in our sleep to do healing work on them. A friend recently messaged me to say that my son and I came into her dream (she has never met my son) and he placed his hand over her third eye and did some healing on it, telling her to "let go". She asked me what this meant and I told her that I remembered it; it had happened and was not a dream.

You see we are all so busy! My son regularly follows me around in spirit while he is at school. I see, feel and talk to him. In fact, I was holding a workshop once and a healer came to me at the end and said, "You do realize you and your son are jumpers." We jump through portals regularly. She said that as I was talking she saw my son appear beside me; he was listening to me, supporting and encouraging me.

The first crystal that helped me realize this gift was moldavite. It captivated me instantly; I was floating above my body in black space, but it felt comforting. I was presented with three doors or portals to past lives and this is when I went back to ancient Mesopotamia to discover more about crystal skulls (page 143).

Crystals that aid astral travel

* Moldavite
* Spirit quartz (see image on page 152)
* Clear quartz – including high-vibrational types: herkimer diamond; brandenberg quartz; ametrine; starbrary (cosmic) quartz; lightening struck and alchemised quartz such as Aura quartz's, aqua aura and angel aura
* Vera cruz amethyst
* Anandalite

You could also work with selenite at your crown to open you up fully.

Tips for astral travel

If you want to have astral adventures of your own, please make sure you are in a safe space and you feel protected. Ask your guides for assistance and protection and please have a lot of grounding crystals with you – black tourmaline, shungite, labradorite, amethyst and obsidian. After astral travel, I feel weightless and dizzy when I ground back into my body. It's important to create a grounding cord (page 56) and let your energies settle before you stand up. And please follow it by drinking plenty of water. The key is to relax and have fun. Don't question it, go with it.

If you don't feel safe, check on your grounding method and ask for more protection. But if you have asked your guides and angels to help beforehand, they will make sure you are safe. Trust that.

Place the crystals suggested (opposite) on your third eye or higher chakras and use your intuition to ask that they open up safe portals for your journey. Depending on your connection to the crystals, this might happen very naturally without you having to prompt, or you may have to walk your soul down a beautiful white tunnel, like the one in the rose-garden meditation (page 88). See huge tunnels of white light in front of you extending up and out into the cosmos. Step into one of them and feel an angel's presence by your side taking you up to where you need to go. Just go with the flow and don't force anything from there; stay relaxed and focused on your breath.

My journey with lightning-strike quartz

Lightning-strike quartz, or lightning quartz as it is also known, is exactly what it says, and it is rare. It's quartz that has been struck by lightning underground with such force that it melts and cracks. The quartz is imprinted with powerful cosmic and raw elemental energy and its super-high vibrations connect and align all the chakras and energy field. It has been found in two regions of Brazil, the Diamantina Plateau in Bahia state and the Minas Gerais region.

Lightning-strike quartz has the power to ground you deeply and also to rocket you up and out of your stellar gateway. Each crystal is very personal; it will do different things for different people.

This crystal speaks of change. It is ready to help you re-align and vibrate to your highest energetic potential. It is a masculine crystal of raw power, which comes from the cosmic frequencies embedded when the lightning bolt struck it. It is a connector, to help you see what you need to see at that time, to feel what you need to feel, with great clarity. The crystal kept whispering to me in a soft voice that it was a key

crystal, which in building terms means that it is the last crystal placed in the arch, and it symbolizes completion.

For me, this means it is the bridge between the ethers – from our higher chakras, the causal chakra, the soul star and the stellar gateway to the cosmos, the divine, the dimensions we cannot see but may feel. I really believe this crystal bridges the gap between these worlds, helping us to travel through them with more ease. "He" – the lightning-strike quartz – tells me he does all of these things, but strong protection is needed alongside him, as you would expect with a crystal of such power. If, full of light, you rush into that infinite, wide-open space, wanting to connect

"Lightning is one of the most elemental forces of nature, but it seems lightning bolts are so powerful they can reshape the atomic structure of rocks they strike. Researchers have uncovered evidence that lightning can not only melt the surface of rock but also alter the crystals beneath in ways only thought to occur in the extreme pressures of meteor impacts. Geologists found the lightning strikes turned the rock into a material known as shocked quartz, which only forms under extreme pressure."

National Geographic, 2015.

with everyone and anything, then you cannot predict or filter what or who comes to you. Such a step needs to be treated with great reverence. Strong grounding crystals, such as black tourmaline, are needed to work alongside this crystal unless you have experience in this cosmic work.

This is nothing to be scared of. In my experience, when such light-filled beings have pure intentions of love, they attract the right beings to them. You may find spirits who have been waiting to connect, who have been with you for many years and you have not known that they have been waiting for this time. They might even be cosmic star beings whom you recognize because you have been working with them on the astral planes already.

The crystal tells me that he will give me what I need. This is something I believe all crystals do for us – give us what we most need at that time.

I must add that this crystal is a powerful earth healer, sending blasts of energy right down to the core for deep healing. After all of the joyous messages I hold the laser point of lightning-struck quartz in my left hand. I feel and see it shocking my energy field into action, like a lightning bolt, waking me up, jolting more life into it, expanding it, activating and cleansing it – much like how I feel it will work on the earth.

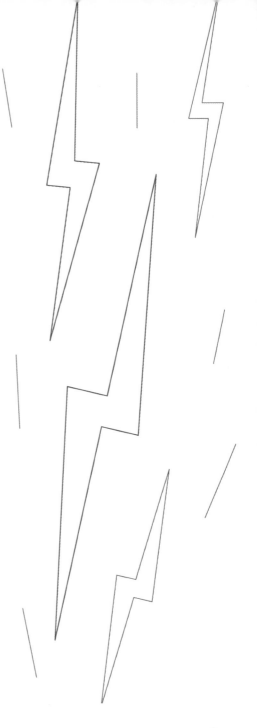

Conclusion

Well, my dear friends, a conclusion feels very final, and this journey is anything but final – it's just the beginning. Your body and its light have been on a journey through these pages, taking in the activations and energy through my words, holding them in your heart and resonating with your soul's blueprint. You may have already heard your crystals speak to you or been given images in your third eye from them. You will have connected to your crystals and their energy because this book is here to give you the space and focus to do so. I don't doubt your abilities and neither should you. Take these experiences and keep journaling, keep writing, keep connecting with crystalline energy and enjoy where the ride takes you, without the pressure of it having to lead anywhere.

I have three wishes for you.

Firstly, I wish you the courage to release any limiting belief systems. That can be difficult with the way society is wired, but there is more out there, more to life, a bigger picture. As for support and guidance, ask the universe and it will be given to you.

Secondly, I wish you the courage to trust your intuition and use it wisely, and thirdly, to be brave in speaking your truth. It's hard, but when you speak out, write and just step up, you inspire others around you to do the same.

I'm really excited for you on this path and I'm supporting you wholeheartedly all the way.

Katie-Jane

Index

Acknowledgements

I would like to thank Mother Earth with the bountiful quarry of gifts that she bestows on us to learn and heal through. Thank you to spirit for guiding me, and to my ancestors for sacrificing so much to get me to where I am now.

To my family. My husband Philip, who has accompanied me through this journey of shoe designer to intuitive healer, never once questioning me and fully supporting me. Simultaneously anchoring me down and holding me up so that I can fly. My little elemental soul Arlo, who boasts to everyone who will listen that I talk to crystals and spirits and that my crystals are in magazines. Well now, my boy, they are in print too. You can do anything you put your heart into. I love you both to the furthest star and back.

Thank you my mother Shirley and fathers: Ian and Richard, earth side and in spirit, and my sister Philippa, for your love and support: even when you do not fully understand what I do, you listen and know how passionate I am about this work.

Thank you to my friend Sarah and her family, Marc, Ann and Debbie. Who kickstarted such belief in myself and the work I do when they invited me to their house in Ireland, treating me like a third daughter and organizing two days of client healing sessions for me to do, you gave me the confidence I needed. I am so very grateful to you.

A big thank you to Stacey at Spiritual Planet for bestowing her high vibe-ing crystals to us to photograph and for being a real sister to me: from the moment we met I knew I had found a kindred heart and a true support.

To friends old and new who have been a big part of my journey and taught me so much.

Thank you to anyone who has come to my workshops or had a 1:1 session with me. In showing up and trusting me, you put your whole soul out there and I value how much courage that can take. I honour you and your journey.

And finally thank you to my Tribe – the friends I have made through Instagram. I wish that I could name you all, but please know that my heart lies with you and I am so grateful for the love and support you have shown me since the beginning of Crystal Muse. This book is for all of you – please know your worth, realize the magic within you, and the potential you have. Keep chatting away to your crystals, keep journaling and keep trusting.